YALE PUBLICATIONS IN RELIGION

DAVID HORNE, EDITOR

PUBLISHED UNDER THE DIRECTION OF
THE DIVINITY SCHOOL

THOMAS-KUCH AWARD OF THE
PRESBYTERIAN
HISTORICAL
SOCIETY

PRESBYTERIAN HISTORICAL SOCIETY PUBLICATIONS

I. *The Presbyterian Enterprise*, edited by C. A. Anderson, M. W.
Armstrong, L. A. Loetscher (Westminster Press, 1956)

II. *The Presbyterian Ministry in American Culture*, by Elwyn A. Smith
(Westminster Press, 1962)

III. *Journals of Charles Beatty, 1762–1769*, edited by Guy S. Klett
(Pennsylvania State University Press, 1963)

IV. *Hoosier Zion: The Presbyterians in Early Indiana*, by L. C. Rudolph
(Yale University Press, 1963)

V. *Presbyterianism in New York State: A History of the Synod and Its Predecessors*,
by Robert Hastings Nichols, edited and completed by James Hastings Nichols
(Westminster Press, 1963)

THE PRESBYTERIANS
IN EARLY INDIANA

HOOSIER ZION

✠

BY L. C. RUDOLPH

NEW HAVEN AND LONDON

YALE UNIVERSITY PRESS

1963

TO ROSE STRADTNER RUDOLPH

PREFACE

I have attempted to make this book more than a log of events or a catalogue of participants in a denominational history. There are several factors that lend special significance to the story of the Presbyterians in Indiana told in the following pages.

The Old Northwest included the territory of the modern states of Ohio, Indiana, Illinois, Michigan, and Wisconsin. One need not subscribe to any doctrine of magic in the free air of the frontier to affirm that this vast public domain was a critical area in the development of America. Among the most crucial questions were those concerning the place of the church. Would the Christian faith be able to keep pace with the new settlement? What sort of Christian faith would it be? Through whom would it come?

Indiana makes an interesting case study because here an unusually strong current of population from the upland South met an especially persistent minority of eastern settlers and missionaries. This encounter of the Hoosiers and the Yankees continues in American Protestantism, though it no longer follows denominational lines. The problems of this adjustment are among the sharper growing pains of the

American Church. The Synod of Indiana provides also a satisfactory unit for observing the procedure and the effects of the Presbyterian division of 1838. All the pathos and rigidity and misunderstanding of this nation-wide split are evident here.

I use "Hoosier" with its original implications of post-revolutionary culture in the back-country South: little education, rural manners, and small tolerance for people who varied in either respect, but this implies no general inferiority or low intelligence of the stock that largely peopled Indiana in her early days. The term "Yankee," broadened a bit from general usage, refers to the culture predominant in the early nineteenth century in the states east of Ohio and north of the Mason-Dixon Line, especially to the settlers who migrated to the Old Northwest determined to reproduce that comparative refinement in the new public lands.

The personnel of the Presbyterian Historical Society, the Indiana State Library, the Indiana Historical Society, and the Indiana Synod Office have been particularly helpful in the course of my research, as have the librarians at Yale Divinity School and at Louisville Presbyterian Seminary. Sydney Ahlstrom, Roland Bainton, and Robert Michaelsen of Yale University have guided and encouraged me during the preparation of the Yale doctoral dissertation that was the first form of this study. Colleagues on the faculty and staff of Louisville Seminary have been generous in reading the manuscript and in their grants of time for study. Special thanks are due the Presbyterian Historical Society for the Thomas-Kuch Award, and to the Ford Foundation, for a grant in assistance of publication.

L. C. R.

Louisville, Kentucky
February 1962

CONTENTS

ILLUSTRATIONS

ABBREVIATIONS

AHMS   Letters to the secretary, American Home
Missionary Society

AHR   *American Historical Review*

CH   *Church History*

HM   *The Home Missionary*

IHSP   Indiana Historical Society Publications

IMH   *Indiana Magazine of History*

JPHS   *Journal of the Presbyterian Historical Society*

MIP   Minutes of Indianapolis Presbytery

MIS   Minutes of Indiana Synod

MLP   Minutes of Lake Presbytery

MMP   Minutes of Madison Presbytery

MSP   Minutes of Salem Presbytery

MVHR   *Mississippi Valley Historical Review*

NS   Presbyterian Church, New School

OS   Presbyterian Church, Old School

CHAPTER ONE ✠ THE SETTLERS

When the glacial ice departed from the land that is now the state of Indiana, it left in the north a belt of fertile till. Meltwater changed the direction of the watercourses, so that they flowed south and prepared there a land of hills, with north-south corridors. Presently, great hardwood forests of elm, beech, hickory, oak, and poplar spread across the wilderness.

The early inhabitants of the modern era, mostly Algonquin Indians, lived in uneasy balance with their eastern enemies, the Iroquois. When the French came to the land, their Jesuits had a dream; and if only the Iroquois, who had obtained guns from New York, had not been so hostile on the route along the upper St. Lawrence and the Niagara; if only the Chickasaws had not been so fierce on the Vicksburg bluffs along the southern route of the Mississippi; if only the Iroquois had not wrecked the mission plans of the Jesuits among the Hurons; if only LaSalle had received more cooperation in his scheme to make the Northwest one immense fur-trading field with the Indians as gatherers—that Jesuit dream might have involved Indiana in a great French Empire.

In the early eighteenth century the white population of Indiana was made up of respectable and licensed French fur traders, less respectable *coureurs de bois* or woods rangers, and Jesuit missionaries. LaSalle's account of his last journey records a sacrifice offered to the Wabash River by the Indians. It was one to delight a Hoosier heart—"some tobacco and beef steaks." Vincennes, Lafayette, and Twightwee Village (Fort Wayne) were established as French posts and Jesuit mission stations. Indiana belonged to the French and the Indians. But for the French it was not a case of finders keepers, and in the maneuvers of the Indians could be traced the influence of two great powers. After 1701 the French had Detroit but the English had New York; the French had better public relations with the Indians but the English offered better prices; the French had Jesuits and woods rangers but the English had persistent settlers. Scotch-Irish immigrants streamed in, filling the back country with land-hungry frontiersmen. For a while, the fur traders of the two powers sparred for Indiana, and war was intermittent from 1749 to 1760. Then the French lost, and Indiana belonged to the English and the Indians.

"Peace" proved worse than war. The whole western country had been ceded to the English without the advice or consent of the Indians, who hated the British. The retiring French traders fed that hatred; and in sullen bitterness the Indians moved to clean out the British outposts, capture Detroit, and push the English frontier back into the sea. In Indiana, Lafayette and Fort Wayne fell before the force of Pontiac's rebellion.

The Chieftain's great plan petered out at Detroit. English traders wanted the Indians to remain, so that they could be exploited. Speculators, including no lesser personages than George Washington and Benjamin Franklin, wanted grants of vast tracts for white settlement. Instead, the English government passed the Quebec Act, which put Indiana along with the rest of the Northwest under the administration of French-cultured Quebec. The passage of this Act was one of the important causes of the Revolution. Eastern colonists had viewed the Northwest as their land for westward expansion.

Now it was the British and the Virginians who sparred for

the Northwest, and with more than fur trade in view. The Virginians, led by George Rogers Clark, won possession. If Clark could have taken Detroit too, the Indiana story would have been much less bloody, but it was to Clark's imperishable glory that he accomplished as much as he did.

The Indians and the Virginian settlers now sparred for Indiana, until the treaty of September 3, 1783, when all Indians on the national domains became wards of the United States. The tribes owned the land, but they could sell to no buyer except the national government. Virginia agreed in that year to cede her claim to western lands to the United States. Indiana and all the Northwest Territory then belonged to both the Indians and the United States.[1]

The nation struggled to treat the Indians fairly, trying to keep white settlers out of Indian territory, as the king had done. But the settlers, contemptuous of Indian claims, jumped the boundary lines in their eagerness to pre-empt rich lands. The Indians with their nebulous organization, had no true representatives who could negotiate for all of them, and their cooperation was spotty at best. English soldiers and traders in the northwestern posts, ready to misinterpret every action of the colonists, incited the Indians to murderous assaults. Finally the United States Government broke the military power of the Indians, paid fairly the claims of the remnants, surveyed the land according to the Ordinance of 1785, provided for new settlements to become units of government within the United States on the terms of the Ordinance of 1787, and sold land to the settlers by providing a series of increasingly liberal land acts. By this procedure Indiana came to belong to the United States and the settlers.

Considerable white settlement of Indiana began about the year 1800. Pioneers then moved in quickly. In 1798 the Northwest Territory could claim an adult white male population of

1. Logan Esarey, *A History of Indiana from Its Exploration to 1850* (2 vols. Fort Wayne, Hoosier Press, 1924), *1*, 80. For a brief description of each of the major Indian families and a map showing their location, see p. 84.

5,000 and so was eligible to name a delegate to Congress. Only two years later Indiana Territory claimed a population of 6,550 and established a new territorial administration at Vincennes, with William Henry Harrison as governor.[2]

Most of Indiana's earliest settlers were from the southern backwoods. It has been customary to think that southern Indiana was settled from the south while northern Indiana was settled from the north and east, the National Road being a rough division. After a painstaking check of census data, Elfrieda Lang concludes that early Indiana was even more southern than most scholars had supposed. Miss Lang's calculations show that in Indiana the southern population moved right on into the north.[3] Indiana was insulated from the northern and eastern population streams by swampy land that blocked the way to the more desirable Wabash country. The lake port at Michigan City was backed by sand dunes, and the persistent "Kankakee Pond" extended from the Illinois line to South Bend. The Yankees bypassed Indiana because they could not, or thought they could not, get in. As Power concludes, "Paradoxically, although the state lay directly in the path of the westward-moving thousands, thousands moved westward and never saw it."[4]

On the other hand Indiana was open to the south. From the Cumberland Gap the watercourses ran northwest. The famous Wilderness Road led to Kentucky and to the Ohio River at points below Cincinnati. Limestone formations and the best soils ran in nearly perpendicular belts northward from the Ohio. These corridors connected Indiana with the Appalachian back country, the great reservoir of land-hungry pioneers.

From these Appalachian valleys came Indiana's early

2. For a precise picture of the population distribution in 1800 see Jacob P. Dunn, *Indiana: A Redemption from Slavery* (New York, Houghton Mifflin, 1905), pp. 295–96.
3. "Southern Migration to Northern Indiana before 1850," *IMH*, *50* (1954), 349–56.
4. Richard L. Power, "Wet Lands and the Hoosier Stereotype," *MVHR*, *22* (1935), 41, 46.

1. MAP OF THE STATE OF INDIANA

a

2. PIONEER HOUSING IN INDIANA: a. Half-faced camp, the first kind of shelter built by pioneers; b. Interior of a log cabin. Note ladder of pegs to the loft

b

settlers. To be sure, a few members of the seaboard plantation stock migrated to the Old Northwest: Charles Willing Byrd, William Henry Harrison, Edward Coles, and the father of Edward Eggleston are examples. There were also population islands, like the French at Vincennes, the Swiss-French wine producers at Vevay, English settlements near Evansville, and the Owen settlement at New Harmony.[5] The towns at the commerce centers quickly attracted and developed a merchant class. But for every handful of these gentry there was a woodsfull of marginal settlers. They may have been Scotch, Scotch-Irish, German, English, or even French in their origin, but they had been pioneering for one or more generations before reaching the Ohio. Their pioneering had been done in the back country of Virginia and especially in North Carolina. The view that the main current into Indiana came from North Carolina is supported by careful students of the population movements.[6]

As a rule the southern settlers were poor. The better lands of Kentucky soon commanded a higher price than new settlers could pay, so they pressed on into Indiana. Though there were few navigable streams reaching back more than forty miles from the Ohio, the settlers pressed across the great river, settled along the available streams, and then assaulted the forest directly. The hills of southern Indiana were not yet exploited or eroded, and the natural drainage provided healthful living sites. Moving to the woods of Indiana meant an outlay of several hundred dollars if one held a Yankee farmer's standard of comfort and equipment. There had to be money for horses,

5. John D. Barnhart, "The Southern Element in the Leadership of the Old Northwest," *Journal of Southern History*, *1* (1935), 187–88. James A. Woodburn, "Pioneer Folk of Early Southern Indiana," *Indiana University Alumni Quarterly*, *23* (1936), 406.
6. Logan Esarey, "The Pioneer Aristocracy," *IMH*, *13* (1917), 272–73. Frederick J. Turner, "Dominant Forces in Western Life," *Atlantic Monthly*, *79* (1897), 434. William O. Lynch, "The Flow of Colonists to and from Indiana before the Civil War," *IMH*, *11* (1915), 1–7. Adolph Rogers, "North Carolina and Indiana," *IMH*, *5* (1909), 49–56.

a wagon, boat transport, land, cabin, barn, and subsistence, both for the trip and until the first crop could be harvested. The great body of southern pioneers had no such standard. They strapped the articles which they felt must be moved upon the backs of their family and animals and set off "jinglety bang." Many had absolutely nothing to lose and were going "no where in perticklar."[7] If they had any money and avoided getting cheated by land sharks, they bought land. If they had no money, they "squatted," hoping to buy later when their situation improved. If their situation did not improve, they became part of that useful group of shifting pioneers who sold their improvements for what they could get and moved on to "squat" and tame more wilderness.

In the woods of Indiana these southern settlers became specialists in subsistence living. Most of them had been "patch farmers" in the back country, and that was what the occasion seemed to demand. There was the perpetual matter of wresting food, clothing, and shelter from the forest and taking care of the family. That was all time permitted. They soon learned that keeping such demands on their time to the minimum allowed more rest for tired and often sick bodies. Their first shelter was likely to be a half-faced camp, a sort of pole pen with an open side before which a fire burned, followed by a rough log cabin. Either may merit description by a traveler as a "pen," a "miserable hole," or a "dirty hovel."[8] William Faux found little to please him on his American tour in 1819, and Indiana frontier cabins were no exception:

> Saving two comfortable plantations, with neat log-
> houses and flourishing orchards, just planted ...I
> saw nothing between Vincennes and Princeton, a
> ride of forty miles, but miserable log holes, and a

7. Lang, *IMH, 50,* 351.
8. Harlow Lindley, ed., *Indiana as Seen by Early Travelers: A Collection of Re-prints from Books of Travel, Letters, and Diaries prior to 1830.* (Indianapolis, Indiana Historical Commission, 1916), pp. 236–37, 256, 291, 301, 312, 527.

mean ville of eight or ten huts or cabins, sad neglec-
ted farms, and indolent, dirty, sickly, wild-looking
inhabitants. Soap is nowhere seen or found in any of
the taverns east or west. Hence dirty hands, heads,
and faces every where. Here is nothing clean but wild
beasts and birds, nothing industrious generally,
except pigs, which are so of necessity . . . Nothing
happy but squirrels; their life seems all play, and that
of the hogs all work.[9]

But even such a warm friend of the West as Richard L. Mason
recorded in his travel account that same year, as he passed from
Louisville through newly settled country to Vincennes, that
accommodations were poor and charges high, the people im-
polite, and their private shelter woefully inadequate to protect
them from the severe weather.[10] In time, if the settler stayed
and prospered, he might improve the first round-log shelter as
a kitchen and attach it by a sort of breezeway to a new and
larger hewn-log house.

When the demands of subsistence living allowed it, the
southern settler did not think leisure a sin. It was a constant
scandal to the Yankee population that the Hoosier made little
hay, planted few fruit trees, built few barns, and seemed content with the most scrubby breed of livestock. Neither the zeal
of the Yankee nor the thrift of the peasant German marked him.
Crawford County farmers climbed the beech and the oak trees
in spring to observe the amount of bloom. If they thought the
bloom forecast enough beechnuts and acorns to fatten their
shoats, they planted little corn.

A host of early writers undertook to characterize the settlers.
Some, plainly resentful, called them ignorant, coarse, lazy,
lawless.[11] Those accustomed to deference because of prestige
or money found the frontiersmen unimpressed by either.

9. "Memorable Days in America," in Lindley, p. 301.
10. "Narrative of Richard Lee Mason in the Pioneer West," in Lindley, p.236.
11. Lindley, pp. 236, 307, 507.

Hoosiers did not call a traveler "sir," they called him "stranger."[12] Samuel J. Mills and Daniel Smith, reporting on their travels through the "Territories," declare, "the character of the settlers is such as to render it peculiarly important that missionaries should early be sent among them. Indeed, they can hardly be said to have a character."[13] On the other hand, some have become romantic about the frontier and its settlers. John E. Iglehart is moved by strong passages from Frederick Jackson Turner's essays, especially: "Western democracy was no theorist's dream. It came stark and strong from the American forest."[14] He overextends the position of Turner and raises a cheer for his favorite team of Methodism and the backwoods man:

> The dominant democracy of America today came from the beginnings of frontier life in the Ohio valley in the society of the children of the wilderness tutored in the schooling of the wilderness, freed from the poisonous European germs existing in the Atlantic coast states from which the backwoodsmen of the Alleghenies and the men of the western waters and their ancestors had fled or been driven into the wilderness. Their Hoosier descendants have come into their own but they also are very slow to recognize the fact.
>
> Methodism came from the southwest to the northwest. A proper understanding of the development of both, in the first three decades of the last century, will show that the itinerant system of Methodism was the handmaid of democracy in the Ohio Valley.[15]

12. Ibid., pp. 66, 527.
13. *The Panoplist and Missionary Magazine*, *11* (1815), 183, cited by R. Carlyle Buley, *The Old Northwest Pioneer Period 1815–1840* (2 vols. Indianapolis, Indiana Historical Society, 1950), *1*, 378. Cited hereafter as *Old Northwest*.
14. Turner, *The Frontier in American History* (New York, Henry Holt, 1920), p. 293. Iglehart gives the wrong location and only a proximate quotation.
15. Iglehart, "Methodism in Southwestern Indiana," *IMH*, *17* (1921), 139–40.

State patriots and historians for local anniversary occasions are also prone to idealize the pioneers.

The way of the frontier farmer was most often hard. He was sick or his horse was lame or the squirrels were eating the corn. But things were about to be different. Every farmer seemed prepared to draw from his pocket a lithographic city and grant the merest acquaintance the favor of taking a few building lots.[16] In spite of present difficulties boundless optimism seemed the mood, and it went with a fierce frontier loyalty that was not anxious for outside counsel. Akin to this was the brashness, buoyancy, and confidence of public figures or candidates—a willingness to support all claims with a fight. The frontiersmen called it a "pushing" spirit and R. Carlyle Buley has attributed to it the ability of young Hoosier doctors to undertake difficult cases without a qualm, and of untried lawyers to plead their cases with unwarranted, flowery eloquence.[17]

The early Indiana settler was willing to share what he had. If there was to be preaching, he would make his house a sanctuary and send out the word—"give out preachin." If travelers needed shelter, they were welcome to the cabin with the rest. In fact, some have charged the Hoosier settler with hospitality beyond his facilities. "Traveled over a fertile country four miles to Steenz, making a distance of thirty-four miles. At this dirty hovel, with one room and a loft, formed by placing boards about three inches apart, ten travelers slept. There were thirteen in the family, besides two calves, making in all, with my friend and self twenty-three whites, one negro and two calves."[18] Problems of dressing or undressing for bed in such large and mixed companies seem to have troubled eastern travelers much more than Hoosiers. For understandable reasons, the settler was willing to share what he had—short of

16. Richard L. Power, *Planting Corn Belt Culture: The Impress of the Upland Southerner and Yankee in the Old Northwest*, IHSP, 17 (Indianapolis, 1953), 49.

17. *Old Northwest*, 1, 387.

18. Mason, "Narrative," in Lindley, p. 237.

his money. This was too scarce. In the new settlements almost all trade was carried on by barter of goods and service. If the store account could be paid in tow linen, "sang" (ginseng), hides, or "chopping," no cash was forthcoming. When a whole acre of bottom land, trees and all, might be had for less than two dollars, parting with silver was parting with one's best hopes for a farm. This has a real bearing on church subscriptions. Cash was not for trade or pledge; it was for land.

Only if he lived beside a heavily traveled road might the woodsman make some charge for accommodations. When he did so, he would most likely add one room to his cabin, hang out a sign to "keep public," and dignify the whole by the name of tavern. The tavern-keeping settler is by no means the typical citizen of Indiana's frontier, however—there were few roads of any importance. "Zane's trace across Ohio had no real parallel in Indiana, and the settlers stuck to the navigable streams with unfailing persistence."[19] The earliest major road in Indiana was the Vincennes Trace or the "Buffalo Trace," from Louisville to Vincennes. It amounted to a westward extension of the Wilderness Road and became the chief land route for southerners bound for Illinois.

In frontier usage the word "route" should usually be substituted for "road." As late as 1823 the route from Vincennes to Indianapolis was laid out by dragging a log with an ox team through the woods, prairies, and marshes.[20] Specifications for roadbuilding were very loose, and there was no effective system of maintenance beyond corduroying crucial stretches with fallen logs. A road was a general indication of direction to which one returned between mud holes. There might be bridges or ferries over major streams, and there might be lodging of a sort along the way. Indiana's roads, or lack of them, called forth some

19. Frederic L. Paxson, *History of the American Frontier, 1763–1893* (New York, Houghton Mifflin, 1924), p. 193.
20. Buley, *1*, 452. For a good concise listing of early Indiana roads see pp. 451–54.

purple passages from early travelers. Baynard Hall, a Presbyterian clergyman and the first principal of the new Indiana Seminary at Bloomington in 1823, commented on the roads only thirty miles north of the Ohio:

> The autumn is decidedly preferable for travelling on the virgin soil of native forests. One may go then mostly by land and find the roads fewer and shorter; but in the early spring, branches—(small creeks)— are brim full, and they hold a great deal; concealed fountains bubble up in a thousand places where none were supposed to lurk; creeks turn to rivers, and rivers to lakes, and lakes to bigger ones; and as if this was too little water, out come the mole rivers that have burrowed all this time under the earth, and which, when so unexpectedly found are styled out there— "lost rivers!" And every district of a dozen miles square has a lost river. Travelling by land becomes of course travelling by water, or by both: viz., mud and water. Nor is it possible if one would avoid drowning or suffocation to keep the law and follow the blazed road; but he tacks first to the right and then to the left, often making both losing tacks; and all this, not to find a road but a place where there is no road,—untouched mud thick enough to bear, or that has at least some bottom.[21]

A critic with fewer clerical inhibitions inscribed in the register book of a tavern at Franklin:

> The Roads are impassable—
> Hardly jackassable;
> I think those that travel 'em
> Should turn out and gravel 'em.[22]

21. *The New Purchase; or, Seven and a Half Years in the Far West* by Robert Carlton, esq. (pseud.), ed. James A. Woodburn, Indiana Centennial Edition (Princeton University, 1916), pp. 49–50.
22. From the reminiscences of J. H. B. Knowland of Indianapolis, cited by George S. Cottman, "Internal Improvement in Indiana" *IMH*, *3*(1907), 20.

In the winter and the spring transportation problems closed Sabbath schools and sharply limited church activities. Any minister who hoped to serve his area—even the most "settled" usually served at least a county—had to arrange for several preaching points within it and itinerate.

The only practicable way to travel was horseback, and that was an adventure. Isaac Reed, Presbyterian preacher and perennial missionary in the Indiana woods, seems always to be deep in mud and water. His saddle girth breaks while he is fording a flooded river, and he narrowly escapes drowning. With his wife and three children he sets out for New York State in May 1826, only to find the roads so bad that the whole family must leave the carriage to make their way through the mud. They wonder if the horse will get through at all. Reed was prevented from attending the General Assembly in 1826 "by the immense rains, which fell about that time." He tells of making his horse swim across flooded creeks; walking a log across, carrying saddle, saddlebags, and coat; catching the horse; and proceeding to the next stream. Small wonder that his description of Indiana in his book has a rather liquid sound: "It is without a mountain, and has scarcely a swamp over which a man cannot ride on horseback. It has much low lands, which at some seasons are wet. Its river banks are low and they overflow widely."[23] Again a folk story best expresses popular feeling: One winter a pioneer found a beaver hat in the road and at the risk of his life waded out to get it. To his amazement he found a man under it and called for help. But the man under the hat protested, "Just leave me alone, stranger, I have a good horse under me, and we have just found bottom."[24]

The typical Indiana settler was often ailing. Theodore Parker, Congregational minister and lecturer, did not see how it could be otherwise. He blamed the "western climate," a sort

23. *The Christian Traveller* (New York, 1828), pp. 89, 177, 217, 233.
24. Variously used of roads and city streets, related by Buley, *1*, 460–61.

of compound of "the fertility of the soil, the dulness of the air, the enervating influence of the physical circumstances." He felt that the American climate had already enervated the Europeans and that the "West deteriorates Americans quite as much. . . . In Indiana I saw but one rosy-cheeked girl, about eighteen or nineteen. 'Were you born here?' 'No Sir, in New Hampshire,' 'I thought so.' I saw 300 or 400 children in the schools at Indianapolis—not one rosy cheek! The women are tall and bony, their hair lank, their faces thin and flabby-cheeked."[25] Observers less prejudiced and less romantic have laid the blame on malaria. In David Chambers' opinion the settlers' most deadly enemy, more dangerous even than the Indians, was the anopheles mosquito, which found ideal breeding places in Indiana's boggy woods.[26] Whatever may have been the chief cause, the pioneer seems to have been more sick than well. He regarded the ague as inescapable:

> There were varieties of ague—dumb ague, shaking ague, chill fever, and so forth. Some had the combined chills and fever each day, or on alternate days, or even every third day; others had the chills one day and the fever the next. Whichever brand was favored, it was regular, but, like the moon, it appeared somewhat later each day; it often came back in season for years, until a sort of immunity was established. Work schedules were planned to accommodate the fits. The justice arranged the docket to avoid the sick day of the litigant, the minister made his appointments in keeping with his shakes, the housewife and traveler planned accordingly, and even the sparking swain reckoned the "ager" schedule of self and intended.[27]

25. John Weiss, *Life and Correspondence of Theodore Parker, Minister of the Twenty-eighth Congregational Society, Boston* (2 vols. New York, 1864), *1*, 327.
26. *A Hoosier History to Accompany the Mural Paintings of Thomas Hart Benton* (Indianapolis, Bobbs Merrill, 1933), p. 17.
27. Buley, *1*, 244–45.

Typhoid epidemics came and went with their cause unknown. Many pioneers called the disease "brain fever" and attributed it to night air, putrid vegetable and animal matter in the air, grief, fear, unripe fruit, want of sleep, and intense thought. Even Asiatic cholera found its way west and killed one-eighth of the inhabitants of Salem, Indiana, in a single week. In short, the settlers had the whole range of common diseases plus some special ones native to their new land. The man who did not want to come to church could use the excuse that the weather was bad in winter and spring and that he was sick in summer and fall. The pious were, of course, subject to the same limitations.

If the Scotch-Irish were champions of popular education when they came to America, their glow for schooling had been considerably dimmed by a generation or more in the American back country. Theodore Roosevelt claimed that the southern pioneer stock must have been of good educational quality because such a small proportion of Tennesseans and Kentuckians appear to have made their signature with a mark. D. D. Banta agreed with Roosevelt and added that the same thing would be found if a large-scale study were made of the documents signed by pioneers of Indiana.[28] However, this is very unconvincing. Some educated and highly trained southerners did come to Indiana. Seventy-four per cent of the members of Indiana's Constitutional Convention were from the South or had been in close contact with that section before coming to Indiana.[29] Settlers in this educated minority were the ones who signed petitions and legal documents and business papers. In addition, some of the small landowners from the Appalachian back country were literate and in some sense educated. But a great mass of the Hoosier population would have had no

28. "The Early Schools of Indiana," *IMH*, *2* (1906), 43. Theodore Roosevelt, *The Winning of the West* (New York, Current Literature, 1905), *3*, 295–300.
29. John D. Barnhart, "The Southern Influence in the Formation of Indiana," *IMH*, *33* (1937), 271.

occasion to sign papers. Squatters might not have signed papers involving land for years, if ever. They might or might not have responded to a military muster.

There had been no system of public education south of the Mason-Dixon Line in the Colonial period and would not be until long after, the prevailing theory being that education was for the upper-class leaders. This was certainly not changed for the better in the Appalachian back country. The remarkable thing was that there were enough private schools and colleges founded there to train some upper-class and professional leaders for a still newer frontier. When Isaac Reed rode out from Virginia in the fall of 1817, he left the Reverend Mr. H. of Rockingham "very anxious that something effectual should be done to supply the back countries of this state with missionaries. They are now deplorably destitute of religious instruction." Reed soon found that the concern of Mr. H. was well founded. He speaks of "very poor human habitations" and "mere hovels, to which the dwellings of the poorest labourers of the northern states seem like little palaces." He says, "We stopped to bait at a hut where there was a hearty man, his wife, and four plump, but dirty children. They were without chairs, and, what is worse, without a Bible, and they scarcely ever heard preaching. . . . The man can read a little; his wife not at all, and there is no school for the children." The route Reed traveled was one of the mountain roads that fed settlers to Indiana. Small wonder that, later, when Reed distributed tracts among the frontier families in Indiana, he found he had to be careful because he was giving away tracts to people who could not read. He finally began to ask bluntly whether they could read before he offered any tracts. He considered the common schools of Indiana in 1827 generally inferior to those of the northern states. He also observed that the state was not divided into districts.[30] Reed, as a true friend of the West, and Mr. H., as a Virginian, can hardly be written off as Yankee libelers.

Richard Power summarizes the statistics from the 1850

30. *Christian Traveller*, pp. 26, 34, 223, 225.

census and concludes that the southern states, which furnished the bulk of the upland population to the Old Northwest, ranked far behind the northeastern states in percentage of the population enrolled in public schools, in public libraries provided, and in periodicals and newspapers published. Significantly, Indiana was lowest among the five states of the Old Northwest in periodicals and newspapers published.[31] Even if it should be conceded that the Appalachian states educated their youth in private rather than in public schools, it would still need to be demonstrated that such privately educated people formed a large proportion of the immigrants to Indiana. The evidence, in point of fact, seems to be in the other direction.

Repeated reference to the low state of education and the prevalence of illiteracy by eastern missionaries must be given credence. Their reports may reflect Yankee prejudice, but it is unlikely that they are lying. Mrs. E. O. Hovey, a missionary bride in a comfortable Presbyterian manse at Coal Creek, quickly discovered "three who live within half a mile of us that do not know a word [of reading], who are mothers of large families and disposed to let their children grow up in the same way, but we hope there is yet some *salt* among us."[32] When the Rev. Caleb Mills of Wabash College began his crusade for free public schools in 1846, his procedure was to hold before the legislature the humiliating facts about illiteracy in Indiana. One-seventh of the state's adults could not read a word, and this figure was determined after a considerable influx of later immigrants from the North and East. In the southern counties of Jackson, Martin, Clay, and Dubois, just a fraction over half of the adults could read and write. Only one-third of the children of school age were attending any school. Indiana rated lowest among the free states in terms of literacy and means of popular education.[33]

31. *Corn Belt Culture*, pp. 39–44.
32. Letter to Martha E. White, Oswego, New York, 12 May 1832.
33. Charles W. Moores, *Caleb Mills and the Indiana School System*, IHSP, *3* (Indianapolis, 1905), 385, 387.

It is no reflection on the courage or versatility of Indiana's early settlers to say that they were poorly educated and that many had no formal education at all. Generations of subsistence living had heightened individualism and self-reliance but had left the people socially impoverished. Crudity of manner and speech became symbols of a folk culture in which each frontier citizen loyally affirmed he was "as good as anybody." Frontier culture had a warm welcome for all who would conform; but it could be cruelly intolerant of those who seemed to differ or to judge its ways. Merrill E. Gaddis describes the cultural lag:

> Frontier people were inclined to depreciate education and culture. . . . A knowledge of American political and military history in its western phases is sufficient to afford one convincing examples of frontier cocksureness, bravado, and feeling of self-sufficiency. The pioneer's ignorance of, and feeling of contempt for, other cultures and other times than his own, led to a reduced appreciation for the beautiful and to a general discounting of refinement in clothes, language and manners.
>
> The frontier attitude toward education is well displayed in a general depreciation of academic training for the ministry, during most of our period, and in some isolated places to the present day. . . . The West had so little education in these early years that it came to disparage formal training as worse than useless. This attitude toward learning was not helped by the fact that the few educated preachers in the West were not infrequently mere formalists who read moral essays without much semblance of spontaneity or warm feeling. Education came to be the synonym for dryness, coldness and impracticability.[34]

34. "Religious Ideas and Attitudes in the Early Frontier," *CH*, 2 (1933), 154, 158. See also Merle Curti, "Intellectuals and Other People," *AHR*, 60 (1955), 259–82.

As a study in cultural regression, consider the family of Abraham Lincoln of Rockingham County, Virginia, "a well-to-do Virginia farmer, who, without the help of slaves, tilled his own fields." In 1776 he "entered" one thousand acres of land in Kentucky and about 1784 moved to Lincoln County there. Soon after, he was killed by an Indian. His elder son, Mordecai, "acquired, in some way, a fair education for a pioneer and could write well." He managed the family affairs. As for the young brother, "no more ignorant boy than Thomas could be found in the backwoods." Thomas' bride was Nancy Hanks, of whom a biographer says, "She was absolutely illiterate." In 1816 Thomas Lincoln, member of the Lincoln family traceable directly to middle-class lineage in England, was baptized a "separate" Baptist in Knob Creek. That same year he set out by raft, accompanied by several barrels of whiskey. "And so, he drifted across and down the Ohio to a landing on the Indiana bank, like a piece of human flotsam thrown forward by the surging tide of immigration." In Indiana, Thomas Lincoln and his family were squatters. They lived first in a half-faced camp, fourteen feet wide. After about a year Thomas Lincoln had built a cabin, the largest the Lincoln family had ever lived in—eighteen by twenty feet. There was no floor, no window, and no door. In 1817 Lincoln was able to make the first payment on his one hundred and sixty acres. The next year Nancy Hanks Lincoln died of a common frontier ailment, the "milk sick." Albert J. Beveridge describes the folks and the folkways of the Lincoln neighborhood so plainly that latter-day Hoosiers have been led to protest. The really remarkable thing is that young Abraham Lincoln, the son of Thomas, was able to go to school at all. One Andrew Crawford operated a primitive subscription school—tuition hams and coonskins—two or three miles from the hut of Thomas Lincoln for one season. By some providence Abraham and Sarah went to school for a while that winter of 1818–19. So when Lincoln was ten, he learned a little simple reading and perhaps how to form words with a quill. When he was fourteen or fifteen, he went to school a bit more, but his schooling totaled less than one year. Thomas Lincoln was typical of the first and shifting echelon of pioneers. There was some refinement as the land was cleared and settlement stabilized, even as there was some cultural improvement in the Lincoln house when widower Thomas Lincoln married Sarah Johnston. But the illiteracy rate of 50 per cent in southern counties as late as 1850 makes rather plain the lack of formal education among the early southern settlers.[35]

Social gatherings in early Indiana were a mixture of the quaint and the crude, the rollicking and the rough. A basic family event most often served as the occasion—a marriage, house-raising, harvest, or funeral. But there might be a crowd at any frontier town for a militia muster, election, public sale, shooting match, or just a Saturday afternoon. Hoosiers of early days were not content to sit and whittle. If the question was who had the best horse, a race was in order. To settle who had the best gun—or the best shooting eye—a match was arranged. Most damage was done deciding who was the best man. If the tests of skill were friendly, a rough system of rules was followed, but as Buley says, the sporting spirit was often lost because the contestants got really mad. Urged on by a tough element, too much whiskey, or bad blood, they began serious fist fights in which scratching, kicking, hair-pulling, biting, eye-gouging, and trampling the downed man were all considered part of a contest that was "fit fair."[36] Fights were easily provoked by any reflection upon the courage, strength, or truthfulness of these frontiersmen. Even such things as neat clothing, correct speech, and a gentlemanly bearing could rouse a bully who disliked what he regarded as effeminacies.[37]

Any frontier occasion—a work party like a corn-husking, or

35. Albert J. Beveridge, *Abraham Lincoln, 1809–1858* (4 vols. New York, Houghton Mifflin, 1928), *1*, 7–59. The protest is reflected in Woodburn, "Pioneer Folk," *Indiana University Alumni Quarterly*, *23*, 401–11.
36. *Old Northwest*, *1*, 318.
37. Benjamin S. Parker, "Pioneer Life," *IMH*, *3*, (1907), 2–3.

a shooting match, or even a revival—might be turned to riot by the consumption of too much corn whiskey. As late as 1820 a teetotaler was a rare thing. Men and women, young and old, sick and well, indulged in summer and winter, in the shop or in the field, on Sundays and other days, at frolics, at elections, at funerals.[38] Both church and court records in Indiana bear out the high rate of drunkenness and mayhem. This would add some cogency to such a standard report as that of eastern missionary Jeremiah Hill in Owen County: "Brother Lowry and myself have 4 places of preaching in Putnam and Hendrakes Counties. Three of these places wickedness prevails to an alarming degree. Drinking, dancing, knocking down and Sabbath breaking in almost every form seems to be the order of the day, but still we have good attendance as to numbers and are gratefully received; in fact we do pray much for revival in each of these places."[39] It is easy to understand the elation of Presbyterian missionary Ashbel Wells in New Albany when he could report that the local temperance society had ninety male members, including five "grocers" who had quit selling whiskey, and that the last election day was not much rowdier than any other day of the week.[40]

Most of the early Indiana settlers were not church members at all. If the Scotch-Irish immigrants were Presbyterian when they came to America, their Presbyterianism was not indigenous to the back country. They did not and perhaps could not produce a church of Presbyterian standards alone on the frontier. Where the pious among the frontiersmen did appeal to the established Presbyterian bodies to the north and east,

38. William W. Sweet, *Religion in the Development of American Culture, 1765–1840* (New York, Scribners, 1952), p. 138. President Joseph F. Tuttle of Wabash College, "God's Work in the World the Last Fifty Years," a discourse preached at Franklin, Indiana, 29 Nov. 1874. See also Beveridge, 2, 51–53.

39. 1 April 1833, AHMS.

40. 5 Jan. 1830, AHMS. For the more usual election procedure see Sweet, p. 139.

their call was met with a mere trickle of missionary itinerants. The commendable efforts of these bodies and the excellent record of some of the missionaries sent out cannot alter the fact. Ernest Trice Thompson states it bluntly: "Ultimately the great majority of the Ulster-Scots were lost to Presbyterianism, if not to the Church of Christ."[41]

The Indiana settlers who were churchmen were likely to be Methodists or Baptists. Both churches had struck fire in the South a generation before Indiana was opened to settlement. They had provided lay preachers where the Presbyterians had provided none. They were the peoples' churches of the southern settlers and thus were the churches of the immigrants to Indiana.

> As a result of the American Revolution the Methodist Church found its first large field of service among the poorer classes of the South. Even more important was the task of saving the new frontiers beyond the Appalachians.
>
> Not only was the conference largely southern in membership but the most fruitful recruiting ground for new preachers, especially in its earlier years, seems to have been the mountain regions of Kentucky and Tennessee. . . . If the people of the South had any peculiar culture, this organization must have been a very efficient instrument in transferring it north of the Ohio.[42]

Baptist preachers outnumbered Presbyterian preachers ten to one by a conservative estimate. Methodist and Baptist leadership was plain in Kentucky, where by 1820 there were 21,000 Baptists, 20,000 Methodists, and 2,700 Presbyterians.[43] Methodists and Baptists were first in numbers and vigor in

41. Gaius J. Slosser, ed., *They Seek a Country: The American Presbyterians* (New York, Macmillan, 1955), p. 79.

42. Barnhart, "Southern Element," *Journal of Southern History*, *1*, 194–95.

43. Robert Davidson, *History of the Presbyterian Church in the State of Kentucky* (New York, 1847), p. 285.

Indiana; they were first on the scene with organized churches. The first Protestant church in Indiana was the Silver Creek Baptist Church at Charlestown, founded in 1798. Methodists formed their first class in the state in 1802 and the Silver Creek Circuit in 1807. The image of the Presbyterian preacher as the outlander, the latecomer, and the "educated big bug" seems to have been on the Indiana frontier from the beginning.

With the Methodist and Baptist churches the settler felt at home; he knew what to expect. The lay preacher was like any other settler except for an added measure of natural gifts and his calling. Peter Cartwright says of the Western Conference that in 1820–21 there were 280 circuit riders, and that among these itinerants there was not one literary man.[44] A native preacher could speak the southern Hoosier language. His preaching was often of the "see-saw-hum-and-spit" variety of western oratory. His illustrations might not hit the theological point squarely but they were in live language which bled when cut. The whole ministry smacked of frontier life. If the lay preacher did not know much about exegesis of the Bible (and few were as keen as Cartwright), he knew how to take almost any text as a basis of his sermon calling men to decision. Thus the patriarch of Ashbaugh Settlement expounded the "speretil meaning" of the account of the good Samaritan by saying, "Some folks think that the two pennies left the Jerickoo man, was nuthin but cash pennies—but my friends, there's a speretil and bettersome idee:—one penny is the law, tother's the gospel."[45] He knew how to condemn the greater evils of thievery, slavery, and drinking whiskey as well as the lesser ones of dancing and playing cards. He was a valuable counselor on ways and means of bearding the devil in a frontier setting because he had wrestled him often before.

The reports of the American Home Missionary Society hold some severe criticisms of the resident lay preachers. Baptists are accused of antinomianism, charged with "substituting mere

44. *Autobiography of Peter Cartwright* (New York, Abingdon, 1956), p. 136.
45. Hall, *New Purchase*, pp. 133–36.

declamation and noise for argument," and labeled as consumers and sometimes as dispensers of whiskey.[46] Moody Chase said there were ten preachers in Orange County when he came, but he wondered whether the people were any better prepared to promote benevolent institutions because of their influence. There were five Methodist preachers residing in Orleans alone but "notwithstanding this great number. . . . when I came here there was no preaching oftener than once in 3 or 4 weeks and no prayer meeting or Sabbath school or Bible Class in the place."[47] Isaac Reed traveled through Kentucky on his way to Indiana and observed. " There are many which wear the Baptists' name, but they have neither the knowledge, order, nor the apparent piety of the Baptists in the northern states."[48] He quoted from a Baptist sermon on heaven, "O my dear honeys, heaven is a Kentucky of a place," and commented that there were thirty who were called Baptist preachers in that county "but there is not, I suppose, a well educated man in the whole number. It has been the burden of their song in these parts, to cry down learning and a salary for a gospel minister, as an abomination not to be borne."[49] A bitter attack against the Methodist preachers in Elkhart came from Noah Cooke:

> The greatest obstacle there to the cause of vital piety . . . is Methodism. About the middle of the winter there appeared much seriousness among the people there and while I was considering whence help could be obtained to commence and continue a series of meetings, the Methodists commenced what they called a *protracted* meeting. This continued a few days and nearly broke down their society. About two

46. James Carnahan, Lafayette, 14 Sept. 1831; James Wheelock, Greensburg, 1 Sept. 1831; J. U. Parsons, Jennings County, 22 Aug. 1832: AHMS. See also Cartwright, pp. 98–99, and Sweet, *Religion in American Culture*, p. 139.

47. 4 Feb. 1833 and 9 April 1833, AHMS.

48. *Christian Traveller*, p. 71.

49. Ibid., p. 48.

weeks since another person of the same denomination commenced a meeting there for the purpose of retrieving the bad effects of the preceding one. . . . An intelligent person, whether an humble Christian or a confirmed infidel, would tell you that the *effect* if not the *design* of the meeting was or is a satire upon the Christian religion and an attempt to bring it into disrepute. I know that many look upon the Methodists as coadjutors in the cause of Christ. But I cannot so view them and were it my dying testimony I should declare that they do much more hurt than good. A vast majority of the infidels that I have ever seen are of those who have once joined the Methodists and then left them under the notion of falling from grace—the Methodists saying that they have fallen from it but they saying if this is it (grace noise and groaning) then there is no such thing as real grace and consequently there is no such thing as grace religion.[50]

In a letter for eastern consumption, with authorization for its use to promote the Redeemer's cause, George Bush praised the zeal of the Hoosier preachers but decried the error-ridden doctrines they expounded and the noisy ranting way they spoke. He also praised the naive eagerness of Hoosier listeners but pointed out that this made the illiterate declamations of the preachers even more regrettable, because the people readily believed anything they were told.[51] There is some reflection of actual woods preaching in Baynard Hall's facetious account *The New Purchase*. He laments the pressure which drives trained ministers from the new settlements.

And if the New Purchasers are abandoned, then must they be cursed out there with *inspired* clergy, such as we have heard thus reciting *their* apostolic creed: "Yes, bless the Lord, I am a poor, humble man

50. Goshen, 1 April 1842, AHMS.
51. Indianapolis, 20 Nov. 1826, AHMS.

—and I doesn't know a single letter in the ABC's, and couldn't read a chapter in the Bible no how you could fix it, bless the Lord!—I jist preach like old Peter and Poll, by the Sperit. Yes, we don't ax pay in cash nor trade nither for the Gospel, and arn't no hirelins like them high-flow'd college-larned sheep-skins— but as the Lord freely give us, we freely give our fellow critturs."

Hall attended a camp meeting at Bloomington in 1824 and reported it in detail. In order to introduce the Methodist minister William Armstrong, Hall tells of a previous preaching duel between Armstrong and a "campbellite Baptist" in which the latter was vanquished. Hall evidences a healthy respect for the ability of this Methodist elder whose aim had now become "to enlarge his own people." But he cannot have had much sympathy for the theme or manner of Armstrong's Sunday morning sermon at the Camp, a rousing attack on Calvin, Calvinists, and Calvinism—"no subject is better for popularity at a camp-meeting." First there is the story of Calvin and Servetus, figuring Servetus as Christian confessor and martyr and Calvin as diabolical persecutor. The whole is done with a voice choir of congregational participation:

Judging from the frequency of the deep groans, loud amens, and noisy hallelujahs of the congregation during the narrative, had Calvin suddenly thrust in among us his hatchet face and goat's beard, he would have been hissed and pelted, nay possibly, been lynched and soused in the Branch; while the excellent Servetus would have been *toted* on our shoulders, and feasted in the tents on fried ham, cold chicken fixins and horse sorrel pie!

Here is a specimen of Mr. S.'s [Armstrong's] mode of exciting triumphant exclamation, amens, groans, &c., against Calvin and his followers:—"Dear Sisters, don't you love the tender little darling babes that hang on your parental bosoms? (amen!)—Yes! I know you do—(amen! amen!)—Yes I know, I know it—(amen, amen! hallelujah!) Now don't it make your parental hearts throb with anguish to think those dear infantile darlings might some day be out burning brush and fall into the flames and be burned to death! (deep groans.)—Yes, it does, it does! But oh! sisters, oh! mothers! how can you think your babes mightn't get religion and die and be burned for ever and ever? (the Lord forbid—amen—groans.) But, oho! only think—only think oh! would you ever a had them darling infantile sucklings born, if you had a known they were to be burned in a brush heap! (No, no!— groans—shrieks) What! what what! if you had *foreknown* they must have gone to hell!—(hoho! hoho! —amen!) And does any body think He is such a tyrant as to make spotless, innocent babies just to damn them? (No! in a voice of thunder,)—No! sister! no! no! mothers! No! no! no! sinners no!!—he ain't such a tyrant! let John Calvin burn, torture and roast, but He never foreordained babies, as Calvin says, to damnation! (damnation-echoed by hundreds.)— Hallelujah! 'tis a free salvation! Glory! Glory! a free salvation—(Here Mr. S. battered the rail of the pulpit with his fists, and kicked the bottom with his feet— many screamed—some cried amen!—others groaned and hissed—and more than a dozen females of two opposite colours arose and clapped their hands as if engaged in starching, &c. &c.) No ho! *'tis* a free, a free, a *free* salvation!—away with Calvin! 'tis for all; *all*! ALL. Yes! shout it out! clap on! rejoice! rejoice! oho-oho! sinners, sinners, sinners, oh-ho-oho!" &c &c.

Hall also gives a full account of the afternoon and evening sermons, and at night he sees Rowdy Bill, the New Purchase bully, stricken down and in mortal combat with the devil while his wife screams "Gouge him, Billy!—gouge him, *Billy!*—gouge him!"[52]

Plainly the Methodist Church had come a long way from John Wesley. And the Baptist Church had come a long way from either its Anabaptist or its Puritan beginnings. The revival had long been a phenomenon of pietism and of the Great Awakening in America. But when it emerged from the Appalachian back country into Kentucky and Indiana, it was something different. Sweet rightly says: "There arose in the West two distinct types of revivalism; the first was the Presbyterian-Congregational type, which might be termed a Calvinistic revivalism carried on under educated leadership. . . . The second type . . . was the Baptist-Methodist-Disciple-Cumberland Presbyterian type whose work was to bring Christianity to the great mass of religious illiterates."[53] But the difference between them was not so much that Calvinism and aristocracy had a crippling effect in the Presbyterian-Congregational type, as Sweet seems to emphasize. The basic difference was between the cultures of the back-country South and the North and East.[54] Evangelical Protestantism had become the folk religion of the Appalachian South, and what proved to be but a traditional phase in the culture of the Northeast became deeply ingrained in the states south of the Ohio River and lasted a long, long time. Ralph Gabriel partly attributes its staying power to the fact that public education developed so slowly in the South and West; therefore, the folk religion had to fulfill the intellectual as well as emotional needs of the frontier people. Illiterate exhorters preached the Bible as they understood it, dwelling not on abstract ideas but on the drama of human conflicts and those between God and the Devil. Open-air meetings lasted late into the night, campfires flickered, religious songs were sung, and the hysterical element in evangelical Protestantism became a commonplace of frontier

52. *New Purchase*, pp. 364–89.
53. *Religion in American Culture*, p. 148.
54. This is the thesis of Richard L. Power in *Corn Belt Culture*.

life. Though romantic and somewhat bizarre, this religion, as Gabriel emphasizes, was completely genuine and very powerful. Its influence tempered the worst evils of frontier living, and it made a deep and lasting impression on American society.[55]

It was democratic in that it belonged to the southern settlers and they did not want it tampered with or criticized. The western-southern revival did not produce crusades to better the world, nor did it send out hosts of missionaries beyond its own people. Rather, it reproduced itself in thousands of camp meetings and became the agency for winning "the great mass of religious illiterates"—the southern immigrants—to the Christian Church. In the providence of God, it succeeded well in this.

There was much Scotch-Irish stock in the southern migrations to the West. Sweet concludes that with a healthy church structure plus this body of Scotch-Irish settlers, "The Presbyterians had the best chance . . . of becoming the greatest of all the American churches both in point of number and influence." This is only partly true. Vander Velde's point is more valid: the Presbyterian Church cannot really be said to have been in the best position to expand in the West if the condition of her expansion was that she no longer be the Presbyterian Church.[56] Presbyterian penetration of the back-country culture was spotty. The Cumberland Presbyterians afford one example of Presbyterian success by partial accommodation; to do even that required a schism. Ministers of the Presbyterian Church were always going away to school; the settlers were going deeper into the woods. This kept the preachers apart from the settlers. Preachers who were different from them were the particular abhorrence of southern frontier folk. Peter Cartwright knew what the settlers wanted: no educated preachers

---

55. Gabriel, "Evangelical Religion and Popular Romanticism in Early Nineteenth-Century America," *CH, 19* (1950), 37–39.
56. William W. Sweet, *The Presbyterians,* Vol. 2 of *Religion on the American Frontier, 1783–1840* (4 vols. University of Chicago, 1936), p. 23. Lewis G. Vander Velde comments in his book review, *MVHR, 24* (1937), 74–75.

who were like lettuce growing under the shade of a peach tree
or a gosling that had got the straddles by wading in the dew;
no hot-house preachers furnished with old manuscript sermons
preached or written a hundred years before; no sapient,
downy D.D.'s.[57] The settlers knew what they wanted: their
own language; illustrations raw and homely;[58] revivals with
plenty of life and conversions; assumption of the superiority of
the common pious man, especially the western man. The
Presbyterians knew in part what the settlers wanted. James A.
Carnahan of Lafayette stated it plainly to the American Home
Missionary Society in 1831: "They want a man that can
preach in the house or out of the house, on a stump or on a
barrel, in a cabin or in a barn. One who if the people cannot
hear him can speak a little louder and if that will not answer,
who can hollow—who must and will be heard. One who can
sit on a stool and lie on the chaff or in a log cabin without
chinking and his wife if he has one must partake the same
spirit."[59] With less sympathy Solomon Hardy of Greenville,
Illinois, wrote the American Home Missionary Society, "I
think . . . that a stout southerner about seven feet and a half
high, with a voice like Stentor, and who could live through the
week on the wind that he had preached out on the Sabbath
would suit them, be his principles and practices almost what
they would."[60]

But the Presbyterians did not give the settlers what they
wanted, and their churches increasingly came to minister to
the educated, and hence the more wealthy, because only the
educated would tolerate an educated ministry. Production of
Presbyterian ministers was so slow that even the comparatively
small demand for them could not be met. By the time of the
settlement of Indiana, after 1800, Presbyterian strength among

57. *Autobiography*, pp. 64, 236, 267.
58. Edward Eggleston said of Cartwright, "His speech was full of dialectic
    forms and ungrammatical phrases. His illustrations were exceedingly
    uncouth": *The Circuit Rider* (New York, Grosset and Dunlap, 1902), p. 72.
59. 14 Sept. 1831, AHMS.
60. 20 Dec. 1830, cited by Power, *Corn Belt Culture*, p. 116.

the migrating southern settlers was small indeed. When Indiana's population was 68,780, there were only four Presbyterian churches in the state, enrolling in all about eighty members.

John M. Dickey, second Presbyterian minister in the state and lifelong servant in Indiana, made a speech for the Home Missions Anniversary in Cincinnati in 1836. He said of the period twenty years before:

> For several years those who were laboring in Indiana, seemed almost to labor in vain. Frequently I was ready to conclude that I was a curse instead of a blessing to the people among whom I labored. Sometimes I thought I was of no use, only to make the hearts of some of the pious who had been long destitute, glad to see something like a Presbyterian preacher. But few were added by emigration, until our brethren in the East began to feel for us, and the prayers of the East and the West met in ascending to the throne of God.[61]

By 1816 Presbyterian missionaries began to come to Indiana from the eastern states.

The conflict was inevitable. Presbyterian ministers were formally educated; Indiana's early settlers were not. Presbyterians felt that trained ministers should be paid; the settlers were now accustomed to lay preachers who served for little or no pay. Presbyterians were enthusiastic about the new reform societies for education, temperance, and morality; the settlers did not care to be criticized or reformed. The Presbyterians were often from the North and East with the speech and manner of that area; the settlers felt a burning loyalty to the West, with a southern complexion. Presbyterians received support from Yankee funds contributed to build a Hoosier Zion; the settlers especially resented Yankee shaping. Presbyterians preached a "baroque" Calvinism (they had also come a long way from Calvin) in an emotionally controlled setting;

61. *HM, 10* (1837), 31–32.

the settlers had largely abdicated theology and associated religion with personal emotional release. This was not a case of religion against irreligion. Both the Presbyterians and the popular denominations among the settlers were preaching evangelical Christianity, with some local lapses on all sides. They were complementary, although they did not behave as if they were. The Presbyterians represented the arrival of ordered and informed evangelical faith on a scene which had generally deserted traditional discipline and education.[62] They did not always present their faith winsomely or effectively, but they dared to be church leaders who would not conform to frontier usage and standards. Perhaps they could not conform to the frontier because they, too, were spokesmen for a culture religion. They deliberately tried to elevate and shape the frontier life, generally into an image of New England. At least the frontier folkways and folk religion had to react to a Christian faith equally valid from a culture very different. The result was wholesome.

Some Presbyterian criticisms of the folk religion have already been cited. These were more than matched by frontier resistance to the Presbyterians, which was very often led by the lay preachers. Opposition frequently took the form of denouncing the societies which the Presbyterians promoted. So it was at Crawfordsville where the Baptist Church passed a resolution prohibiting any of its members from becoming subscribers to a temperance society, and a Baptist minister living near that town declared himself ready to oppose any of the benevolent institutions of the day.[63] Even a Baptist agent (from Ohio) for the American Bible Society got no support at all from his fellow Baptists in Princeton, Indiana. They "utterly disown him almost without exception, and will in no way assist to forward the cause." Religious instruction of any kind and especially by Sunday schools was attacked by the Baptists

---

62. Carlton Hayes, "The American Frontier—Frontier of What?" *AHR*, 51 (1946), 199–216.
63. Claiborne Young, Boone County, 8 March 1833, AHMS.

there.[64] Jeremiah Hill reported that there were about thirty preachers in Owen and Green Counties in Indiana "all of them nearly to a man opposed to Missionary operations, especially to the movements of Presbyterians."[65] Organizers of a Sabbath school in Indianapolis were charged with receiving salaries for their services and exploiting the children through the price of books. It was also charged that the teachers got a commission for every scholar enrolled because the rolls were sent to England where every scholar named became a subject of the King of Great Britain.[66] At Jeffersonville a local physician and Baptist preacher not only violently opposed a temperance society but also any Sunday school, Bible society, tract society, or missionary education society on the grounds of "union of church and state" and infringement of the peoples' liberties.[67] James Crawford reported from Jefferson County, Indiana, that religious sects were numerous "and all harmoniously unite in decrying education as requisite to a public teacher and in abusing the learned clergy who take wages for their services."[68]

Sharpest of all was the opposition to missions. The Baptist churches often attacked missions in their own denomination for reasons difficult to fathom. John Taylor, Daniel Parker, and Alexander Campbell were among the antimission crusaders. But all the "irreligious and sectarians" were suspicious of the American Home Missionary Society and others who sent out Presbyterians. They objected that the clergy were thus made independent of the people.[69] Consider the plight of Archibald Craig, whose house burned and family expenses mounted. His congregation was happy with his work but felt it could not raise its subscription. Nor, as a matter of principle, would it allow him to apply for missions aid. "I must pay for periodicals,

64. Calvin Butler, Princeton, 14 Feb. 1831, AHMS.
65. 22 Feb. 1831, AHMS.
66. *Centennial Memorial of First Presbyterian Church, Indianapolis* (Indianapolis, The Church, 1925), p. 210.
67. M. A. Remley, 14 March 1831, AHMS.   68. 31 Jan. 1827, AHMS.
69. Samuel T. Lowry, Greensburg, 20 Dec. 1830, AHMS.

support benevolent institutions, settle with the postmaster and stationer, pay taxes, discharge the bills of a schoolmaster, tailor, shoemaker etc., etc., out of $170—one half paid in produce and part of the other half paid in nothing at all in order that my people may convince the world that I do not preach for money."[70] In northern Indiana Daniel Jones said of Kosciusko County, "While the great mass of the inhabitants of this region feel and manifest all unconcern about religious matters which might be expected in unregenerate men placed in their circumstances, they have a strong prejudice against the Presbyterian Church, and look with much jealousy and suspicion on the operations of the Society by which I am sent."[71] At the other end of the state Calvin Butler reported:

> Against Presbyterians there is as real a persecution as ever existed under Nero or any other tyrant, though not carried forward in the same manner; and in this the light of eternity will show that the influence of the Methodists, and of some others, is united with that of infidels and unbelievers. There is a deadly hatred towards Presbyterians because they are the firm advocates for the different benevolent institutions existing in our country; and this hatred breaks out against any who bear the name and especially against the office-bearers.[72]

70. Franklin County, 2 Feb. 1831, AHMS. For another instance of a church neither paying the salary nor allowing a request for aid, see John Morrill, LaPorte, 10 July 1834, AHMS.   71. 25 April 1836, AHMS.

72. Evansville, 16 June 1834, AHMS. The record of hostility to eastern Presbyterians is impressive. For examples see the following AHMS: S. Lowry, Greensburg, 1 Sept. 1830; E. Kingsbury, Vermillion County, 25 March 1831; J. Crawford, Delphi, 2 May 1831; U. Maynard, Union County, 9 Aug. 1831; J. Shields, Greencastle, 16 Sept. 1831; J. Wheelock, Greensburg, 10 May 1832; J. Crawford, Delphi, 10 July 1832; C. Butler, Evansville, 4 June 1833 and 13 Sept. 1834; S. Lowry, Putnam County, 27 Aug. 1833; M. Remley, Columbus, 28 Nov. 1833; W. Olmstead, Evansville, 16 Dec. 1833; J. Todd, Marion County, 4 Feb. 1834; M. Chase, Orleans, 11 Aug. 1834; C. Cory, Lima, 1 Oct. 1834; J. Stocker, Delphi, 9 Sept. 1836.

The Presbyterians were under merciless pressure to conform. Often they gave up one post to move to another. Moody Chase left the work at Paoli saying, "The greater part of the town and vicinity are Quakers. Another part Methodists another infidels. And a very few—some four or five families—Presbyterians. I could not keep a S. School in operation. And some of our people had heard that I was a New School man and under the H.M.S. away off to the East there. And it seemed to me that it was not best to fish where there were so few fish and they among so many rocks."[73] But conform they did not. Their strength was that of standing against the southern backwoods culture and their weakness was their lack of real communication with that culture.

The Presbyterians grew more numerous in Indiana nevertheless. Wherever they had ministers to send, they did well among the already loyal Presbyterians, the Yankee settlers from the North and East, the upper-class farmers, the professional men, and the townspeople. These, and their natural increase, made a considerable congregation for Presbyterian efforts. In some places they reached the poorer southern settlers, but this was not typical. Even if Presbyterian ministers preached to them, the prevailing prejudice was generally enough to prevent their becoming members. James Crawford of Delphi tells of ministering to newcomers, of preaching to them in their cabins. They listened respectfully and promised to start a Sabbath school, but Crawford's real hope of educating these frontiersmen lay in a plan to import poor people from the East, who could seek their economic opportunity in the West while serving him as teachers in the Sabbath schools.[74] It was a common notion to import easterners to leaven the southern lump.

The slow spread of Presbyterianism was not a result of automatic Arminianism in the forest.[75] To argue this, one must

73. 11 Aug. 1834, AHMS.   74. 10 July 1832, AHMS.
75. Sweet, *Religion in American Culture*, pp. 210–11; and *Story of Religion in America* (New York, Harper, 1939), p. 317.

hold that the success of the Baptists on the frontier depended on their keeping their Calvinism secret. The awesome aspect of the forest, the helplessness of man before the weather and disease, the ever-present suffering and death would argue as well for a natural Calvinist theology as a natural Arminianism. When the frontiersmen were Arminian, it was because the most effective of the folk churches, the Methodist, sprang from the Anglican Church when the body was Arminian. It was reinforced on the frontier by revivalism, which, when long continued in an extreme form, undercuts theological maturity as well as church doctrine and practice. "Revivalism thus tends to lean theologically in an Arminian or even Pelagian direction with the implicit suggestion that man saves himself through choice."[76] The highly effective system of circuits manned by gifted professional itinerants among people of a like background and culture explains the spread of Arminianism and of Methodism on the Indiana frontier.

Nor is it tenable to hold that Arminianism and Methodism are the particular handmaidens of democracy because so many frontiersmen obviously chose them.[77] The theoretic connection of Calvinism and democracy has been as ably advanced. Such a view of Arminianism and Methodism as the particular vehicles of American democracy depends upon a theory that American democracy was made on a particular western frontier, "stark and strong from the American forest." This is highly questionable, although church historians seem to hold the idea more tenaciously than others.

> Our successive American generations of frontiers-
> men on the eastern seaboard, in the piedmont, across
> the Alleghenies, along the Ohio, the Great Lakes,
> and the Mississippi, over the prairies, and into and

76. Sidney E. Mead, "Denominationalism: The Shape of Protestantism in America," *CH, 23* (1954), 301.
77. Iglehart, "Methodism in Southwestern Indiana," *IMH, 17*, 138. Sweet, *Religion in American Culture*, pp. 97, 115; and *Story of Religion*, p. 319.

beyond the Rockies, may have thought of themselves as Americans first. They may have adopted Indian dress and Indian usages in hunting and fishing and scalping. They may have exerted, and doubtless did exert, a profound and lasting influence on the nationalist evolution of the United States. But all this did not make them Indians or immunize them against the superior and eventually mastering civilization which emanated from Europe and relentlessly followed them. They remained Europeans and retained at least the rudiments of European civilization. After all, the American frontier, as Professor Turner so ably and perhaps regretfully showed, was an evanescent phenomenon, ever passing from primitiveness toward the social and intellectual patterns of the area in back of it. In other words, the abiding heritage of traditional civilization outweighed . . . the novelties acquired from Indians and wilderness. Continuity proved stronger than change. The transit of culture was not so much *from* as *to* the frontier.[78]

The main body of southern settlers did not choose their church because it was Calvinist or Arminian or democratic. They responded to the superb work of traveling preachers in seeking them out. The Methodists and Baptists did not condemn the settlers; they sat where the settlers sat and sought conversions. When later missionaries dared to judge the culture, both the settlers and the lay preachers stoutly resisted.

78. Hayes, "American Frontier," *AHR, 51*, 206. See also Arthur Schlesinger, "What Then Is the American, This New Man?" *AHR, 48* (1943), 225–44. Norman W. Spellman, "The Turner Thesis and Its Significance for American Church History" (special-study paper for "The Literature of American History, 1954", MS in Yale University Library), p. 39.

CHAPTER TWO ✠ THE PREACHERS

Most of Indiana's early Presbyterian preachers were educated Yankees. To be sure, they might have protested the title, because they did not all come from New England; but they bore the marks of eastern education. Whether they were sent by the General Assembly or by an eastern missionary society, they were agents of a body "away off there." They were trained more or less according to the standards of Europe or of the eastern seaboard. They were examined according to a procedure recognized by Presbyterians everywhere. And they were received as members of a presbytery which was a fellowship of ruling elders and ministers, a governmental unit, a veritable trade union of educated clergy.

Some came to Indiana as pastors following the settlers, often at the invitation of some former parishioners now transplanted to the wilderness. Some came as missionaries of the General Assembly, sent in answer to the pleas of the people for pastors or supplies, and some as missionaries of the eastern missionary societies. Whatever the source, they felt that a normal ministry was a settled ministry in which the formally trained minister taught and disciplined and shepherded his people as a closely knit and responsive community.

In these terms Indiana could only be a mission land.

The first two Presbyterian preachers assigned to Indiana did not go. They made their excuses to Transylvania Presbytery meeting at Hardin's Creek, Kentucky, on 5 October 1803, after that Presbytery, earlier in the year, had directed them to visit Indiana in response to appeals from the settlers.[1] It was to have been entirely an extra-duty assignment without expenses paid. Neighboring pastors might make some effort to care for the missionary's parish while he was away, but that was the extent of the presbytery's contribution. The failure of Archibald Cameron and James Vance to fufill their assignment is a symbol of the ineffectiveness of the regular Presbyterian channels in supplying a ministry for the frontier. Their excuses were probably quite valid and were as a matter of record sustained by the brethren of the presbytery. But the settlers in Indiana were still unchurched and unserved. Even if these two missionaries had fulfilled their appointments, they would probably have made only one brief horseback tour to "supply the destitute." They would have reported to the presbytery that their assignment had been completed, and the whole procedure would have begun again in consideration of pleas from the settlers.

Indiana was at first within the bounds of Transylvania Presbytery, which counted its main strength in Kentucky. Most settlers came into Indiana through Kentucky. It was natural that some Presbyterian preachers from south of the Ohio crossed the river to visit the new settlements. Dickey's classic history states: "In the years 1804–1806, short missionary excursions were made in the vicinity of Vincennes by the Rev. Messrs. Samuel Rannels, Samuel B. Robinson, James McGready [of Great Revival fame] and Thomas Cleland, members of Transylvania Presbytery, Kentucky. The immediate fruits of those labors were the gathering and organization ... of the first Presbyterian Church in Indiana, which was

1. "Minutes of Transylvania Presbytery" (Louisville Presbyterian Seminary Library), 3, 70, 75.

consequently called after the name of the territory."[2] These men were visitors and travelers.

Thomas Cleland has left the first clear record of Presbyterian preaching in Indiana. Transylvania Presbytery meeting 9 April 1805 records that "a petition from a number of inhabitants of Knox County, Indiana Territory, praying for supplies was presented and read." Two days later the record says, "Mr. Cleland was appointed to supply in Indiana territory as much of his time as he can with conveniency,"[3] Cleland was frontier trained and an unabashed revivalist. He was soon to become the most popular Presbyterian preacher in Kentucky, notable for such measures as preaching without notes and shortening the five-hour sacramental service by dispensing with tokens and serving communion elements to the people seated in the pews.

Describing a visit to Indiana in the spring of 1805, Cleland points out that Transylvania Presbytery had no northern or southern limits and that the country he journeyed through was a destitute wilderness. He was rewarded for his hardships by being welcomed at Vincennes, where he was to conduct services, by young William H. Harrison, then governor of the Indiana Territory:

> The first sermon I preached—and it was the first ever preached in the place, at least by a Presbyterian minister—was in the council-house, but a short time before occupied by the sons of the forest. I preached, also, in a settlement twenty miles up the Wabash, where were a few Presbyterian families, chiefly from Shelby County, Kentucky. They were so anxious to

2. John M. Dickey, *A Brief History of the Presbyterian Church in the State of Indiana* (Madison, 1828), pp. 11, 12. Indiana Synod's historian Lucien V. Rule has asserted in his enthusiastic way that Samuel Shannon was probably the first Presbyterian preacher in Indiana and that Shannon in turn sparked the interest of Archibald Cameron (1803), James Kemper (1804), John Todd (1806), James McGready, and others to visit the new territory. He does not provide documentation. See his unpublished manuscript, "Samuel Shannon, Giant of God" in Indiana State Library.

3. "Minutes of Transylvania Presbytery," *1*, 106, 109.

> have me settle among them that they proffered to send
> all the way to Kentucky to remove my family, without
> any trouble or expense to myself, besides offering me
> a generous support . . . . And though I was prevented
> from settling among them . . . yet for a number of
> years afterward I received messages from those who
> claimed me as their spiritual father.[4]

Harrison seems to have been a politique in religious matters,
giving equal favor to all. The governor himself held the candle
at service for an early Methodist preacher at Vincennes.[5] At
another time he was host to Father Stephen Badin and a warm
friend of Father Jean Rivet of the Roman Catholic Church.
Harrison also sought and obtained government support
for Catholic missions among the Indians of Indiana Territory.[6]

Charting the earliest Presbyterian preachers in Indiana
makes plain that the General Assembly was the first eastern
benefactor. In 1802 the Assembly had formed the Standing
Committee of Missions, to report how many missionaries the
available funds would employ, to nominate the missionaries to
the Assembly, and to handle the reports from the field. There
was never much money—less than $2,500 per year from 1802
to 1811 for the whole Assembly—and there were always too
many calls for the resources. The committee tried to stretch its
money as much as possible by paying very little and making
very short-term appointments, generally one to six months.
Schermerhorn states that it took the Presbyterian appointees
half their time to get to the field and return. When they arrived
on the field, they found it so large they could do little more than
ride through it one time, speaking where they had the oppor-

4. *Memoirs of the Rev. Thomas Cleland* (Cincinnati, 1859), pp. 87–89, 103.
5. William W. Sweet, *Circuit-Rider Days in Indiana* (Indianapolis, Stewart, 1916), p. 9.
6. Thomas T. McAvoy, *The Catholic Church in Indiana, 1789–1834* (New York, Columbia University, 1940), pp. 98–99, 116–18.

tunity.[7] The Assembly's Committee of Missions deliberately chose the policy of wide itineration and held fast to that policy throughout the early years of Indiana's settlement;[8] but even with the widest itineration, the Assembly had almost no riders for Indiana. Up to 1815 the General Assembly had commissioned eleven missionaries to Indiana for periods of from one to four months. They were Samuel Scott (1806–07), James Dickey (1807), Stephen Bovelle (1811), James McGready (1811–16), William Robinson (1813–14), Thomas Williamson (1805), Samuel Holt (1806), Thomas Cleland (1806), Daniel Gray (1815), Joseph Anderson (1815), and James Welch (1815).

Only two of the Assembly's early missionaries located in Indiana. Samuel Scott served for nearly twenty years as teacher and preacher at Vincennes and died there in 1827. William Robinson moved to Madison to teach in 1814. The next year he organized the Presbyterian congregation there and stayed to strengthen it until 1819. For the next eight years he lived at Bethlehem, so afflicted with a "dropsical malady" that he could do little.

Robinson was remarkable among the Presbyterian preachers of Indiana. He was a Scotch-Irish preacher of the Old School who had studied theology with Samuel Finley in Kentucky. Ravaud K. Rodgers, a young missionary from Princeton with credentials from the General Assembly, found Robinson had no sympathy with either his theology or his mission in 1819. In the matter of whiskey, Robinson is quoted as saying others might preach against it if they pleased, but as for him, he would drink it.[9] And he did—as a regular habit and at times

7. John F. Schermerhorn, *A Correct View of That Part of the United States Which Lies West of the Allegany Mountains, with Regard to Religion and Morals* (Hartford, 1814), p. 43.

8. Colin B. Goodykoontz, *Home Missions on the American Frontier* (Caldwell, Idaho, Caxton, 1939), p. 157. Clifford M. Drury, *Presbyterian Panorama: One Hundred Fifty Years of National Missions History* (Philadelphia, Board of Christian Education, 1952), pp. 27–31.

9. Dickey, *Brief History*, pp. 5, 12. Hanford A. Edson, *Contributions to the Early History of the Presbyterian Church in Indiana* (Cincinnati, 1898), pp. 52, 59, 128.

to excess. But despite his drinking, he was an enterprising man who set up business with a cording machine that he erected.[10] The mission society preachers who soon took leadership in Indiana were total abstainers, promoters of missions, and opposers of secular occupations for the clergy. Robinson would never have understood.

The Assembly knew that its itinerant policy was a makeshift but felt it could do neither more nor less. Schermerhorn observed that little or no good could arise from such missionaries.[11] John Dickey looked on the Assembly's itinerants from his point of view as a contemporary resident minister in Indiana: "It is to be lamented . . . that from the brevity of the commissions given by that body, and the extensive field of operations they must embrace, the good effected has been by no means proportionate to the time and treasure expended."[12] Edson considered three Assembly missionaries in 1815 to be little more than "mere horseback riders," whose labors were too transient to achieve significant results.[13] Efforts of the regular presbyteries and synods, even that of the Synod of Pittsburgh or the Western Missionary Society, could not maintain a trickle of assistance to Indiana's need.

The progress of the Presbyterian Church in Indiana to 1815 is disappointingly slow. Small congregations were gathered at Vincennes (1806), Charlestown (1807 and again in 1812), Washington (1814), and Madison (1815). One may plead the hindrances and disorders of the war, but it is necessary to note that these did not stop progress of settlement. Samuel J. Mills gives the best picture of the situation in 1815:

> Indiana, notwithstanding the war, is peopling very fast. Its settlements are bursting forth on the right hand and on the left. In 1810 there were in the terri-

10. James B. Lewis, "The Pioneers of Jefferson County," *IMH*, *12* (1916), 217.
11. *A Correct View*, p. 43.
12. *Brief History*, p. 18.
13. *Contributions to Early History*, p. 61.

tory 24,500 inhabitants; now they are computed by
the governor at 35,000, by others at 30,000, and by
some at 50,000. Its principal settlements are on the
Miami and Whitewater, on the Ohio (extending in
some places twenty miles back), and on the Wabash
and White Rivers. Many small neighborhoods have
received an addition of from twenty to forty families
during the last summer. When we entered this territory there was but one Presbyterian clergyman in it,
Mr. Scott of Vincennes. He was valiantly maintaining
his post there for six years past. He has three places
of preaching, and although he has not been favored
with an extensive revival, yet his labors have been
blessed to the edification of his congregations. His
church consists of about seventy members. Between
the forks of White River there is also a Presbyterian
congregation in which there are about thirty communicants, and we have lately heard that a clergyman has settled among them [Dickey had preached
there but he was not yet settled]. In the State of Ohio
we saw the Rev. William Robinson. He informed us
that he expected soon to remove to the territory and
establish himself at Madison on the Ohio. It is prob-
able, then, that there are now three Presbyterian
clergymen in the territory. But what are they for the
supply of so many thousands? They are obliged to
provide principally for their own support, by keeping
school through the week or by manual labor. They
have therefore very little time to itinerate. The settlements on the Miami and the Whitewater we did not
visit, but were informed by missionaries who have
occasionally labored there that they afford promising
fields of usefulness. Probably congregations might be
formed there. Places of preaching where considerable numbers of people would assemble might be
established with short intervals from Lawrenceburgh,

near the mouth of the Miami, to Jeffersonville on the Falls of the Ohio. In the vicinity of the Falls are two other flourishing little villages, Charlestown and New Albany. It is of high importance that the standard of truth should be immediately planted there, for these places or some of them must soon become rich and populous towns. At Charlestown there is a small Presbyterian Church. But it languishes for want of the bread and water of life. Leaving the river and proceeding a little further west we came to other flourishing settlements. Corydon is the present seat of government for the territory. Salem, a county seat, has near it three other places where churches might be formed. These settlements are yet in their infancy. It is said, however, that they are able to support a minister. And yet there are people here who for five years past have not seen the face of a Presbyterian clergyman.[14]

Samuel J. Mills was also the prophet of a new day. The General Assembly had not been able to send him on this western tour, so he arranged to go for the Massachusetts Missionary Society. He made his report to the world, but especially to the eastern missionary societies. And from those societies came the vigor to establish the Presbyterians in Indiana. As Sweet has observed, the revivals in the Presbyterian colleges supplied the leadership for frontier Presbyterianism, particularly south of the Ohio, in the same way that revivals in the Congregational colleges of New England furnished leadership for the frontier regions north of the Ohio.[15] It was the "wise men from the East," backed by the missionary societies, who put strength into the Presbyterian program in Indiana after 1815. Missionary societies recruited and supported

14. *Report of a Missionary Tour through That Part of the United States Which Lies West of the Allegheny Mountains* (Andover, Mass., 1815), pp. 15–16.
15. Sweet, *Religion in American Culture*, p. 148.

eastern seminary graduates to work in Indiana. They aided pastors already in the field. They cooperated with the auxiliary Indiana Missionary Society in a kind of strategy for the field—the eastern societies sent out the men, and the Indiana Missionary Society assigned them to crucial places. In his history published in 1828, John Dickey offered a list of the early ministers which even then included a dozen missionaries from the societies. He readily acknowledged Indiana's debt to the Christian benevolence of several distant societies, especially the Connecticut Missionary Society and the United Domestic Missionary Society of New York.[16]

There had been a long history of cooperation between Congregationalists and Presbyterians. They had both been dissenters from the state church in England and in 1690 had actually agreed to merge their operations there under the name of United Brethren. There were many Presbyterians among the early Puritan settlers in America, and New England church government often had a Presbyterian look, the Saybrook Platform of Connecticut (1708) being an excellent example. When the need arose for ministers for the West, it was natural that Presbyterians and Congregationalists should work together. They approved the Plan of Union in 1801. Under this plan Congregational ministers could serve Presbyterian churches, or Presbyterian ministers could serve Congregational churches wherever that was convenient. There were generous provisions for representation in church courts and for church discipline.

Indiana's settlement had been just beginning in 1801 when the Presbyterians and the Congregationalists entered into their Plan of Union for joint operation in the West.[17] The effect of this was to make the college and seminary graduates of the Congregational schools available for "destitute" Indiana. They were sent out with Presbyterian and Congregationalist money

16. *Brief History*, p. 18.
17. For the exact wording of the Plan see "The Plan of Union of 1801," *JPHS, 10* (1952), 94.

through the mission societies.[18] Since so few of Indiana's settlers were from New England, these eastern missionaries founded Presbyterian churches under the Plan of Union. By 1850 there were but three Congregational churches in the whole state and one of them was the congregation at Bath, Indiana, a Presbyterian splinter group which had borrowed the Congregationalist name.[19] Isaac Reed's history is an interesting example of how Presbyterianism was furthered on the frontier by one with Congregationalist backgrounds. Reed attended Middlebury College in Vermont, was taken under the care of Long Island Presbytery in New York, and was licensed by the Fairfield Congregational Association in Connecticut. He served under various eastern societies, including the Connecticut Missionary Society and the American Home Missionary Society. Reed founded more churches than any other eastern missionary to Indiana—all of them Presbyterian churches!

It is fascinating to speculate on the motivation of these eastern societies and their missionaries to Indiana. In their calls for funds back East they made a bald appeal to political security, suggesting that new states were being carved out of this western empire and their representatives would one day rule the land; New England might be outnumbered and she had better see to it that this new West was both wise and good:

> Facts place the subject beyond a doubt, that within a generation to come, the millions of the Atlantic states will be under the stern necessity, by the federal compact of this Union, to surrender their destinies to the outnumbering millions who will soon throng the Mississippi valley . . . Should the United States continue to populate for years to come, with a rapidity

18. Goodykoontz, pp. 149–51. Frederick I. Kuhns treated the whole united work in his dissertation "The Operations of the American Home Missionary Society in the Old Northwest, 1826–1851," University of Chicago, 1947.

19. Moses Wilder, 21 Nov. 1836, AHMS.

equal to years past, there will then be a population in this country, within an hundred years of 320,000,000. Such in general is the superiority of soil in that great valley, that a given portion of land is capable of sustaining three times greater amount of population, than the same portion in the Atlantic states. Hence there is reason to believe that the excess of population in the valley, over the Eastern section, will exceed within a century the expectations of those who are at present most sanguine in their calculations.[20]

The call to frontier adventure must also have been a real factor at work on the young seminary graduate. If a commission from a missionary society could allow him to tour the great West, serve an apprenticeship in preaching among the destitute, and at the same time pay off his educational debts, a licentiate found it attractive. A real concern for the unchurched was a prime mover among these missionaries, especially in the early nineteenth century, when widespread revivals heightened the concern. Crucial as any motivating factor was a kind of Calvinistic meddlesomeness, a special variety of community concern, maybe more basic to historic Calvinism than technical theories of predestination or the decrees. The easterner had come from a more genteel culture, even more lately improved by temperance societies, Bible societies, tract societies, and Sunday schools. Whenever he saw or even heard about the mud and illiteracy and grossness of the frontier, the need overwhelmed him. He felt the call as one of the elect to do something about it. Perhaps the most persistent theme of the frontier missionary letter was "building up Zion." It was progress in building Zion that the executive secretary of the society wanted to hear about. It was for this cause that eastern capital would flow. The purpose of the missionary in Indiana was building up Hoosier Zion—a segment of the kingdom of

20. Benjamin C. Cressy, *An Appeal in Behalf of the Indiana Theological Seminary Located at South Hanover, Indiana* (Boston, 1832), pp. 5, 15.

God. This was to be done for the good of every man, even if some men did not like it. Certain pressures ought to be brought to bear on the common life of all. Everything must give way before God.

When one considers that as late as 1846 the uncouth frontier preacher Peter Cartwright was running for national Congress against another unpolished frontiersman, Abraham Lincoln, it is not hard to understand the Yankee concern. Also both religion and morals needed help on the frontier. The Wild West (the term originates on the Wabash) was destitute of "sound and proper" religious institutions. "The Home missionary movement was the resultant of many forces: Christian idealism, denominational rivalries, humanitarianism, nationalism, and enlightened self-interest all had their effect in producing and directing a movement designed to mold the West according to orthodox Protestant standards."[21]

First there was a tendency to proliferation in missionary society work. Indiana received missionaries from the Connecticut Missionary Society, from the Young Men's Missionary Society of New York City and from others as well. Then came consolidation. Several societies in the State of New York combined in 1822 to form the United Domestic Missionary Society. By 1826 this body had 127 missionaries, four of whom were in Indiana.[22] That year the United Society combined with the Connecticut Missionary Society, the Massachusetts Missionary Society, and others to form the American Home Missionary Society. "At the outset most of the financial support for the Society came apparently from Presbyterians. Of the $20,000 received in the second year (1827–28), $16,121.27 was credited to New York and only $1,641.34 to four New England states." The American Home Missionary Society grew mightily until in its tenth year its receipts were over $100,000. That year 191 of 755 missionaries were in the West and twenty-four were serving in Indiana.[23]

21. Goodykoontz, p. 39.
22. Edson, p. 257.
23. Goodykoontz, pp. 179–80.

The American Home Missionary Society never sent many men into the South. The missionaries were from New England or the Middle Atlantic states and disliked slavery. Officers of the Society found that missionary operations in the slave states were more expensive and less fruitful than in the Northwest. Among the states of the Northwest, Indiana was the most "southern" and proved the hardest field for the American Home Missionary Society. Calvin never had it so hard in Geneva as some of the Presbyterian missionaries had it in Indiana. "Exotic" is the literal word for Presbyterian ministers in early Indiana. It was not that they had lost out; they had never really been there at all. Now they came late and mostly from the East, entering as Yankees into the hog and hominy belt. If the Appalachian settlers were culturally limited, it led them not so much to regret their limitation as to demand that their churches conform to it. These frontiersmen had no basic aversion to doctrine, but it had to appeal to their ego and be presented movingly "in a storm."

Presbyterian missionaries looked upon the Indiana frontier as a great sea of destitution. They were shocked and often showed it with condemnation. They tried to preach traditional doctrine only to find that a favorite sermon of the backwoods preacher was a denunciation of all "biggity" and educated preachers who were assumed to hold themselves above the people. The missionaries proceeded at once to organize temperance societies, Sunday schools, Bible societies, and missionary auxiliaries, only to find that folk resentment could solemnly declare all these to be not only unnecessary but an affront to God.[24] They tried their hand at community reform and were promptly accused of alliance of church and state. Presbyterian ministers on the Indiana frontier were not original shapers of tradition. They arrived late and their number was small. Upon arrival they met an exclusive revivalism and

24. For the amazing story of antimissionary activity among Indiana churches see John F. Cady, *The Origin and Development of the Missionary Baptist Church in Indiana* (Franklin, Indiana, the College, 1942); Buley, 2, 466–67.

folk "frontierism" already occupying the land. Whenever the Yankee preacher and the southern settler met in Indiana, the shock was mutual. Some of the preachers stayed at their work, though the field was "like plowing upon a rock." Missionaries were often shoddily treated. Nothing short of an ideal of Zion could have kept them going.

Just because the lot of the missionary was so hard there, Indiana did not get her numerical share of the missionaries sent. The missionary societies were inclined to bypass Indiana in favor of northern Illinois or Michigan or Wisconsin, where Presbyterians were more appreciated. This was simply a matter of spending mission funds at the point of greatest opportunity. Alert Indiana missionaries were quick to notice the policy. Benjamin Cressy of Salem wrote to the American Home Missionary Society that he felt they were actively favoring Ohio and Illinois over poor Indiana as a promising missionary field.[25] Moses Wilder made the same point:

> I intend *Deo Volente* to write some things about Indiana shortly in order to remind you that "there is such a state as Indiana" and that while it has almost double the population of Illinois it is receiving but little more than half the aid, and has only about the same number of ministers. Illinois is supposed to have 375,000 inhabitants and Indiana 700,000. Illinois has 70 ministers and Indiana 76. In 1833 three years before Illinois had 38 ministers and Indiana 72 ministers. Why is this?[26]

Missionaries to the Hoosiers were often discouraged. By the time of the Civil War they felt they had made very little impression on Indiana. It is true that growth seemed slow and progress small, but they were building better than they knew.

The Presbyterian Church has never really occupied Indiana,

25. 6 June 1831, AHMS.
26. Bath, 21 Nov. 1836, AHMS. See also M. Wilder, 8 Feb. 1837; M. Post, Logansport, 31 Oct. 1836; S. Lowry, Crawfordsville, 20 Oct. 1836; J. Johnston, Madison, 8 July 1825: AHMS. *HM*, *9* (1836), 193-224.

but the fact that she exerted any considerable influence in the state at all is due largely to the missionary societies and especially to the American Home Missionary Society. This body sent Presbyterian ministers to fields in Indiana where there had been none before. On any roster of outstanding Presbyterian pioneers must be the names of James Carnahan, James Chute, James Crawford, Benjamin C. Cressy, John Finley Crowe, John M. Dickey, E. O. Hovey, James H. Johnston, Solomon Kittredge, Samuel Lowry, Caleb Mills, Martin M. Post, Isaac Reed, and John Todd. These are the giants, and they were all at some time missionaries of the American Home Missionary Society in Indiana. They were the leaders in missionary statesmanship and directors of Presbyterian affairs in the state. The method of the American Home Missionary Society became the method of building Hoosier Zion. The techniques of the Society were both resented and imitated by the General Assembly's Board of Missions. It is not entirely a biased view which Joseph S. Clark, Secretary of the Massachusetts Home Missionary Society expresses to William Badger, Secretary of the American Home Missionary Society, 29 April 1844, "There is not a church in Indiana of the Presbyterian or Congregational order that did not spring from missionary efforts. The same is true in Iowa, only one or two in Wisconsin, less than a dozen in Illinois, and not more than twenty in Ohio that do not owe their origin to home missions. Strike out the American Home Missionary Society and you strike the sun from the heavens."[27] The missionary societies sent some men born and educated in the East, like the "polished preacher" Benjamin C. Cressy to Salem, the successful minister to youth Solomon Kittredge to Bedford, and pioneer preacher Martin M. Post to Logansport. They sent some western-born seminarians back West with a commission. Such a one was Philip S. Cleland of Kentucky who, after studying at Andover Seminary, returned to serve over twenty-five years in Indiana.

27. Cited by Frederick I. Kuhns, "The Breakup of the Plan of Union in Michigan," *Michigan History*, 32 (1948), 166.

They commissioned some resident Indiana pastors to spend part of their time in missionary itineration. Isaac Reed spent much time on such missionary labor to the benefit of both his family budget and Presbyterianism in the state.

Every missionary of the American Home Missionary Society got a commission with plain instructions. It stated the amount of support to be given for the year, usually renewable only upon request of a congregation showing cause for continued aid. The credentials of the minister must be acceptable to the church body in whose bounds he worked. Quarterly reports from the missionary were expected to precede the quarterly payment of support and so came in promptly. Thousands of these are extant in the files of the American Home Missionary Society papers. The reports describe the encouragements and difficulties of missionary life. They report regular additions to the churches. Because both the American Home Missionary Society and the General Assembly actively promoted the benevolent causes of the day, missionaries reported their progress in forming Sunday schools, increasing Sunday school libraries and recruiting scholars. A typical report was submitted by Lucius Alden:

> There are associated in the Aurora Sabbath School Union 18 schools, containing 190 teachers and 1068 pupils. Each school is furnished with a Library containing in all 2526 books . . . The influence exerted by these schools has been of the highest importance. A number from them have been united with churches of different denominations within the last year. When I entered this country 3 years ago not one of those schools was in operation nor had a Sunday School library ever been known among our citizens.[28]

Archibald Craig said that some boys in one of his Franklin County Sabbath Schools recited each Sunday from 200 to 300

28. Rising Sun, 13 July 1829, AHMS.

verses and within the first two months almost twelve thousand verses had been recited.[29] At Evansville, J. R. Barnes wrote that he was eager to see a full generation that had been Sunday-school trained; he was sure that no mob leaders or lynch-party members would be among those who had had a full course of religious instruction.[30]

D. C. Meeker reported a problem: "The exact number of books which may be called available to the Library I cannot state, and for this reason, the scholars for the most part have been very irregular. All who have come have taken books and many seem to have come only for that purpose and after receiving the book were not careful to return it. In this way the books have been scattered and as it seemed unavoidably. This renders it impossible to state the exact number, but I think it was about 200."[31]

The eastern missionaries were total abstainers and glad to promote the temperance reform. Almost every quarterly report gives the local reform status. That of Leander Cobb of Charlestown is typical: "The Temperance cause is becoming a subject of increasing interest among us. Most of the members of our churches adopt the principle of total abstinence from the use of ardent spirits and the Clark County Temperance Society has within the last three months had an accession to its number of more than two hundred members."[32] Missionaries put on the pressure of law whenever they could. Sometimes they acted to make the cost of a liquor license prohibitive. Daniel Jones of Warsaw wrote that he had persuaded the commissioners to raise the license fee from 15 to 50 dollars.[33] By 1847 there was the possibility of local option. A. L. Kedzie wrote from Goshen that state legislature had authorized the different towns to decide whether they would have license given for the retail of liquor, and, though strong efforts were made against them,

29. 14 Aug. 1830, AHMS.
30. 1 Feb. 1842, AHMS.
31. Lima, 29 Feb. 1848, AHMS.
32. 17 April 1835, AHMS.   33. 16 May 1838, AHMS.

53

Kedzie's group carried the *No License* ticket by a large major-ity.[34] For this the Presbyterians were accused, with some justice, of joining the powers of church and state. Other charges descend to the ridiculous. Moody Chase was solemnly ques-tioned at a public meeting of the Temperance Society about whether or not he received a premium for every name given to the pledge.[35] It became the practice to press the cause of temperance on July 4th, because to keep the people soberly occupied on that day was an accomplishment.

Organization of local Bible societies, tract societies, educa-tion societies, and mission societies was reported with rejoicing. The missionary often gave a detailed word picture of his parish, counting the number of sermons delivered at his preaching points and the number of Bible classes in operation, reckoning the proportion of time used in visitation and the extent of participation in the "concert of prayer" for missions. Early reports from Indiana were likely to register the genuine mutual shock of New England preachers encountering Hoosier settlers. However, as the quarters passed by, the reports tended to become stereotyped, and finally a chart or "schedule" was prepared for listing the statistical information in columns.

The American Home Missionary Society and its antecedents intended to support a continuing community ministry in the West. They felt an occasional ministry was ineffective. One or more congregations would be aided in support of a resident minister in the hope that they would soon come to full support and aid the cause of missions to others. However, these congre-gations might encompass preaching points that included one or two counties and so represent a sort of localized itinerary. Agents of the American Home Missionary Society, as differ-entiated from missionaries, itinerated more widely to encourage congregations and to formulate missionary strategy. At the same time, the Indiana Missionary Society, an auxiliary of the American Home Missionary Society, commissioned some itinerants to minister in vacant churches.

34. 12 April 1847, AHMS.   35. Orleans, 18 Nov. 1834, AHMS.

Because the American Home Missionary Society contributed substantially to the salary of frontier ministers, those
ministers were expected to spend full time in ministerial duties.
Farming, merchandising, or even teaching was frowned upon.
These were not unworthy occupations, but for a missionary
they were diverting. At the point of full support for a settled
ministry the Society flew in the face of frontier folkways and
earned for its men the frequent epithet "hireling." Nevertheless,
the Society upheld its position that its missionaries should give
themselves entirely to the work of the ministry and avoid over-
frequent changes of parish. "You seem to regret my frequent
changes of location and say that 'nothing more discourages the
efforts of the Society than the frequent changes of ministers.'
No one is more sensible of the evil tendency of such changes,
than I am; or more deeply deplores the necessity of having to
make them; yet such is the heterogeneous character of society,
and the fluctuating state of things here in this 'far West' that
changes of this kind are often unavoidable however undesir-
able."[36] By 1829 the Assembly's Board of Missions had adopted
a similar policy of supporting a settled ministry rather than
appointing itinerants.

The societies knew how to make use of the printed page. The
Massachusetts society had its *Massachusetts Missionary Magazine*; the Missionary Society of Connecticut had the *Connecticut
Evangelical Magazine.* For the first two years of its work the American Home Missionary Society used the *New York Observer* as its
paper, but in 1828 a new monthly magazine appeared, *The
Home Missionary*. Its aim was to develop a missionary constituency to send aid to the West. It also served to keep the need
for missionaries before the seminarians. Reports from the
western missionaries made the finest kind if motivating material:

> Some of our towns and villages contain cultivation
> and refinement, with the means of grace ably adminis-
> tered; but in most places there is an alarming destitu-

36. M. A. Remley, Columbus, 28 Nov. 1833, AHMS.

tion of intelligent, discriminating preaching. We say, "intelligent and discriminating," for with the Catholics, the Campbellites, the Universalists, and the sects the burden of whose proclamation is invective against an educated ministry, there is no lack of preaching any where. This fact, however, increases rather than diminishes the obligation of intelligent Christians to render us assistance. "If the light be darkness, how great is that darkness!"[37]

Tho' a soul in itself considered is worth as much in New England as one in Indiana, yet taking into account the sphere of influence in which both will probably be called to act, and the consequences upon posterity . . . the conversion of a young man or woman in this country, apart from the intrinsic value of the soul, is worth more than ten conversions at the East.[38]

One thing is certain. We all must be a great deal more awake to this cause of missions in the West, or all is lost. Infidelity will get possession of the largest & fairest portion of these United States. This is already coming in upon us from the Old World like a flood occupying this outpost. I give the alarm & call for help. I have done it before & so have others. We look to our brethren in Eastern States for help.[39]

The field is large and important and at present we are like the valley in Ezekiel's vision, full of dry bones and the Lord God alone knoweth whether these dry bones will live or die; By turns we both hope and fear, Brethren pray for us, and for the spiritually dead around us.[40]

Because the reports were specific, they were rather hazardous. When western citizens read the magazine, they might recog-

37. *HM*, *17* (1844), 74.
38. James Wheelock, Clinton, 6 Jan. 1836, AHMS.
39. Asa Johnson, Peru, 3 Nov. 1841, AHMS.
40. J. Woodruff, elder at Lima, 19 Dec. 1833, AHMS.

nize themselves as not very flatteringly presented! Moody
Chase wrote that the settlers in his area, feeling they had
been portrayed unfavorably in a recent report, were furious.
He assured them that he was willing to emend anything un-
true or incorrect, and he noticed that since the incident the
people were taking pains to be sure they had preaching every
Sunday, whether or not Chase himself was available. They
appeared to fear the reports of a Presbyterian minister,
especially if he had come from the East.[41] The files of the
American Home Missionary Society papers show how gener-
ously the editor of *The Home Missionary* used his blue pencil
before he published reports from the field.

The General Assembly's ventures in publication were disappointing. The *Evangelical Intelligencer* (1805–09), the pam-
phlet *Missionary Intelligence* (1810), and the *Missionary Reporter*
(1829–32) had, none of them, a long or satisfying life.[42]

Thus the societies marshaled the resources of the East.
Offerings of Bible classes, "female cent societies," congrega-
tions, and individuals were channeled into the work. Caleb
Mills was being backed in his Indiana mission work by the
Ladies Association of Pepperell through the American Home
Missionary Society. Samuel Foster at Bloomington was to re-
ceive $200 provided for this specific work by Worcester, Massa-
chusetts. One of the few light notes in the American Home
Missionary Society correspondence came when John Thomson
got assigned to report to two sponsors at the same time.[43]

The greatest difficulty about the work of the American
Home Missionary Society was its independence from the
regular structure of any denomination. It really belonged to
the Congregationalists and the Presbyterians and was supported by them, but in missionary activity it dwarfed both of them.
The General Assembly's Board of Missions never attained the

41. Moody Chase, Orleans, 8 July 1833, AHMS.
42. Drury, *Presbyterian Panorama*, pp. 37, 84.
43. Mills, Crawfordsville, 10 May 1834; Foster, 20 Oct. 1835; Thomson,
 Crawfordsville, 25 Feb. 1836; AHMS.

stature of the American Home Missionary Society until the Old School–New School division. No matter how earnestly the guidance of the Indiana Synod and her presbyteries was sought, the Society had the final say concerning which requests for aid should be granted. Thus the secretary and agents did wield immense power. No matter how the Society might urge proper relation to local church bodies, missionaries were paid by the Society and reported to the Society. The Society was likely to be their first loyalty. Sidney Mead cites a contemporary opinion that the secretary of the American Home Missionary Society actually wielded more uncontrolled power than the whole college of bishops presiding over the Episcopal Church of the United States.[44] This situation was somewhat alleviated by creation of the Indiana Missionary Society auxiliary to the American Home Missionary Society. This body recommended and very nearly directed the placement of American Home Missionary Society men in Indiana.

> The judicious and speedy location of the missionaries whom you may send, we regard as a matter of great importance, and we wish to be able to exert a beneficial agency in regard to it. We have many vacancies and they are widely scattered, and it does not appear advisable that every missionary should make it a point to visit them all or even a large number of them before he makes his selection. Such a course has in one or two instances been pursued, and the effect upon the congregations and upon the missionary himself has been found to be by no means a desirable one. The fact is, it ought to be distinctly understood beforehand that there is nothing, at present, very inviting but many things, quite the reverse, in most of the situations, in this state, where we wish your missionaries to be placed. Whoever comes hither with

44. "Evangelical Conception of This Ministry in America," in *The Ministry in Historical Perspective*, ed. H. Richard Niebuhr and Daniel D. Williams (New York, Harper, 1956), p. 215.

the expectation of finding a place exactly to his mind, and with the determination not to locate himself till he meets with such a one, will doubtless, after making the tour of the state, go out where he entered, and return disheartened "to the land from whence he came." No missionary, in this region, ought to be governed, in his views, by present appearances. In most cases an experiment needs to be made, and considerable labor bestowed, before he can determine with any degree of probability respecting his ultimate prospects.[45]

Requests for American Home Missionary Society aid were most often sent through the Indiana Missionary Society for approval. Even so the Indiana Missionary Society was not the Synod and was itself a symbol of independence.

Missionaries were often lax about taking their places in the presbytery. J. W. Wheelock was in the parish at Greensburg for a year before "joining" the presbytery, and even then he never allowed the presbytery to exercise any approval or disapproval over his pastoral relation. Samuel Hurd wrote that Wheelock was considered as sent by the Home Missionary Society and was kept in the parish in spite of the members and the presbytery.[46] W. W. Woods attended the presbytery very little, even when urged, and was prone to make pastoral arrangements without consulting his brethren.[47] In 1832 Madison Presbytery noted the divisive situation and proposed two solutions:

We believe that the proposition made at the late convention for a Western Board of Missions under the control of the Gen. Assembly is one which ought to have been acceded to. We think that such a Board ought to satisfy those who prefer ecclesiastical super-

45. James H. Johnston, Madison, secretary of Indiana Missionary Society, 13 June 1827, AHMS.
46. Samuel Hurd, Greensburg, 21 Dec. 1833, AHMS.
47. Ransom Hawley, Bloomington, 20 Aug. 1838, AHMS.

vision and that most of those in the West who prefer
voluntary associations would cheerfully acquiesce in
such a plan as most likely to allay present collission.
It is moreover our opinion that a great part of the
jealousies and difficulties now existing might have
been avoided if Presbyteries had carefully attended
to the directions in the Form of Gov. Chap. 18th and
that every Presbytery ought to have the whole direction and control of all missionaries within its bounds,
whether sent by voluntary associations or by Boards
under ecclesiastical supervision.[48]

But no solution was effected short of division of the Presbyterian Church. The fault lies as largely with the presbyteries as
with the American Home Missionary Society. They were
unable or unwilling to exercise careful oversight of either the
churches or the ministers in their bounds. Some of the presbyteries gladly abdicated their responsibility and left mission
matters to the American Home Missionary Society; some of
them bitterly resented the fact that the American Home
Missionary Society did what they as presbyteries were failing
to do.

Baynard Hall jokes about the eastern mission societies and
their greenhorn missionaries to the West, but he pays tribute
to those "true missionaries" in the New Purchase as very excellent men. He praises their self-denial, zeal, tireless labors, and
disinterestedness, and observes that though they were considered Domestic Missionaries they endured as much as their
brethren in foreign fields, and without the incidental excitement
and support derived from foreign mission work, especially when
the woods preacher came to depend for his entire sustenance on
two or more weak settlements once the aid of the missionary
society was declined or withdrawn.[49] Hall has no sympathy
with eastern attacks on secular employment for the clergy. He

48. Extract from MMP, 4 April 1832, furnished by James H. Johnston,
stated clerk of presbytery, to Absalom Peters, New York.
49. *New Purchase*, pp. 120–21.

says such employment was the woods preacher's only hope of getting any money at all. As an alternative he suggests a new society, "The-make-congregations-pay-what-they-voluntarily-promise Society,"[50] because he found that most clergymen were doing all they promised and more but the congregations were not.

John Dickey's average annual salary for his first sixteen years in Indiana (1815–31) was eighty dollars.[51] Mrs. William Martin remarked to a guest at the Martin House in 1823 "that for seven entire years she had never seen together ten dollars either in notes or silver."[52] Isaac Reed asked the presbytery for release from Bethany Church in 1825. Among the reasons for moving was the fact that he had not received a dollar in money from his congregation for almost two years.[53] The American Home Missionary Society put pressure on western congregations to pledge at least half a minister's support (generally $400 per year after 1830) before the Society would give aid for the remainder.[54] One of the first things a young missionary had to learn was that the congregational part of this pledge was likely to be made with "Kentucky enthusiasm." It would be paid in part with produce and in part not at all.[55] Most settlers did not have cash. As missionary Samuel G. Lowry phrased it, "Money is not to be had for anything that people have got."[56] Besides, the settlers were always being harangued about the unfitting association of wages and the clergy. Many missionaries agreed with what Moses Wilder reported in 1834, namely that the Baptists and Methodists had served these Indiana areas until even they became disheartened. Their ministrations had left no mark on the people

50. Ibid., pp. 59, 123.
51. Edson, p. 65.
52. Hall, p. 58.
53. *Christian Traveller*, p. 158.
54. Goodykoontz, pp. 182–83.
55. Charles T. Thrift, "Frontier Missionary Life," *CH*, 6 (1937), 113–18.
56. Putnam County, 27 Aug. 1833, AHMS.

except a determined prejudice against supporting the clergy. This grew to the point where the entire income of Methodist circuit preachers for a full quarter was only $5.50. It was small wonder they left the circuit.[57] Ulric Maynard, having encountered the same prejudice, expressed the wish that he were some sort of craftsman so that he might make the Gospel available without charge to these people who needed it but were against supporting it.[58] But such enthusiasm would hardly fill the need. Samuel Lowry of Rockville became so hard pressed that he had to request a missionary barrel: "We have 8 children. The first four sons 20–18–16 and 14 years of age. The oldest 3 I have had at college. The 2nd has just graduated. The next 3 are daughters 12–10 and 8 years old. The next a son near two years old. Besides these I have a widow sister with three children that I have to provide for. She has two sons 8 and 5 years and a daughter 6 years old. I shall not say what kind of clothing I want. There is no kind that can come amiss in such a family."[59]

The plain impression is that Indiana's early Presbyterian churches were quick to seek mission aid and slow to leave it. To accede to the cries for more missionaries was only to increase the need for support. The churches founded were too weak to support a ministry but too important to neglect entirely. Over the years the mission societies paid the larger share of salaries. In 1837 Moses Wilder provided a summary of the situation in Indiana. He stated that there were eighty-five Presbyterian and eleven Congregational ministers, seventeen of whom were teachers and eight others secular businessmen. Only thirty-two preached to a single church, many to two churches, and some to three or more. Only eleven of the churches were able to support ministers without aid.[60] Asa Johnson had a theory to explain such small progress, which he voiced in 1841 when he applied for renewal of his commission at Peru. He felt

57. Jefferson County, 5 Feb. 1834, AHMS.
58. Liberty, Union County, 7 Nov. 1829, AHMS.
59. 15 Aug. 1842, AHMS.   60. Bath, 30 Oct. 1837, AHMS.

definitely that there was a difference in the kind of people who were settling Michigan, Illinois, and other new states from the kind who had come to the Indiana Territory; had the latter been like the former, the Indiana churches would have been independent long ago.[61]

In the West as in the East, a young man aspiring to the Presbyterian ministry was expected to prepare himself in the liberal arts, in Bible, and in theology. The rule was not rigid on how he got his preparation; the presbytery was to supervise that training and ascertain by examination that he had gotten it prior to his licensure or ordination. For example, James H. Johnston was honor graduate of Hamilton College in New York and completed the full course at Princeton Seminary. He was licensed to preach at the opening of his last year in seminary after examination by Columbia Presbytery. Then he went as a missionary to Indiana under appointment of the Domestic Missionary Society of New York, and after further examination was ordained by Salem Presbytery in Indiana. On the other hand, William W. Martin took his whole course of study in the town of Paris, Kentucky. He began with five years of study in John Lyle's academy and finished with two more years of theology under the same John Lyle. West Lexington Presbytery licensed and ordained him. Later he served thirty-two years in Indiana, organizing eight churches and operating a famous "log college" preparing others for the professions. Any candidate for the ministry was examined first on his experimental acquaintance with religion. Unless he was a graduate in liberal arts he could expect to be examined in the arts and sciences from astronomy to logic. In addition he must be prepared in theology, church history, sacraments, and church government, and in Hebrew, Greek, and Latin. There were usually set parts for the trials, including a Latin treatise, an interpretation of an assigned portion of scripture, a lecture on a theological subject, and a popular sermon.

61. 3 Nov. 1841, AHMS.

It would be easy to overstress these requirements. As a matter of fact the Latin treatises appear to have been on a limited number of subjects. "De Satisfactione Christi," "An Sit Christus Vere Deus," "De Natura Christi" are examples of favorite treatise subjects in Indiana presbyteries. Most of the examination parts followed a familiar pattern in which the candidate and the examiners cooperated. Unless some problem was disturbing the church or unless the candidate was obviously unprepared, the examinations were a kind of demonstration among friends, an initiation into the fellowship. The ideal of an educated Presbyterian ministry was somewhat battered upon arrival in America, and it suffered further under a triple pressure: there was a severe shortage of ministers; many men wished to enter the ministry but would not or could not earn the degrees; many men already in the pastorate were not graduates and judged matters accordingly.

Prior to 1811 a Presbyterian candidate for the ministry usually studied theology under the tutorship of some active pastor, and did so while residing in the pastor's home. There were no standards to which these private pastor-tutors could be held, and each was a law unto himself. There are numerous tales and some clear information about many of these tutors and their methods. In general they put primary stress on memorizing the correct opinions about theology. A number of them had as text-books hand-written copies of "divinity lectures" which they had copied out themselves years ago as students. Another favorite method was to hand the student a long list of theological questions for which he was to work out the orthodox answers. Biblical and historical subjects were badly slighted. Preaching and pastoral care were learned by example from the pastor-tutor. Books were very very few, and often very old and out-dated.

Inadequate as this sort of education was, it did

manage to keep alive in the better men the desire for a genuine education. By 1805 some Presbyterians were urging that a theological school be established. Eventually, in 1811, the General Assembly agreed to do so, and chose Princeton as the location. During the next 25 years Presbyterians founded two more seminaries in New York state, one in Virginia, one in Pennsylvania, one in Kentucky, one in Ohio, and one in Indiana.

Yet the older order died hard. In a letter written to a friend in 1829 a Princeton Seminary professor poured out his troubles. Very few students took the whole seminary course. Many stayed only one year in seminary, and some even left after one term. And, he wrote, the presbyteries licensed and ordained these men without even asking the seminary faculty how the men had done in their studies. The newer seminaries founded after Princeton were in no better position. . . .

The Church as a whole and the seminaries strove to maintain a relatively high standard, but many candidates entered the ministry without formal training in both college and seminary. An "educated ministry" meant in practice that which any given presbytery could be induced to accept in a specific case.[62]

Still, the Presbyterian preachers did look bookish on the frontier. Some were very well educated. Comparatively speaking, they all were. A Baptist critic has said that this made them unsuited to the field in which they were to labor. In his opinion the long schooling of the Presbyterians had emaciated their bodily powers and rendered them incapable of enduring the hardship of the backwoods. In short they were charged with

62. Leonard J. Trinterud, "Theological Education—Then and Now," *McCormick Speaking*, 8 (1955), 12–13. For a description of a promising young man "lassoed" for the ministry, sketchily prepared in theology, and kindly examined, see Cleland, *Memoirs*, pp. 68–87.

acquainting themselves with books rather than with men and with adapting their manners to the cultivated few rather than to the illiterate mass.[63] But the Presbyterians generally ignored this sort of advice and continued to "tie all their knots high in the air."[64]

Even if the educational standard was poorly kept, there was no inclination to dispense with it. Indiana presbyteries did not complain about high standards for the ministry; they championed the standards and kept urging each other to meet them. When the president of Miami University in Ohio proposed to recruit Indiana students for his three year predivinity course instead of a regular college degree, Johnston ran the news in the *Indiana Religious Intelligencer* as interesting but without approval.[65] Isaac Coe, an outstanding ruling elder at Indianapolis, gave his opinion to the American Home Missionary Society concerning the cultural gap between the missionaries and the settlers. He regretted that correctness in doctrine had lost ground because of this difficult situation, and that the early Presbyterians who came, knowing more about books than men, were not able to unscramble quickly the error taught to these people by the lay preachers of the South and West, who had more knowledge of how to appeal to the feelings and prejudices of the Hoosiers than of how to teach them right doctrine.[66] His conclusion, however, urged better identification with western men rather than a lesser educational requirement.

Indiana was mostly woods in 1831, but there was no apology for a thoroughly educated ministry that year when Salem's Benjamin C. Cressy preached at Hanover:

> How absurd to suppose that it is either pleasing to
> God or profitable to men that the weak minded and

63. John H. Spencer, *A History of Kentucky Baptists from 1769–1885* (2 vols. Cincinnati, 1885), *1*, 559.

64. James H. Johnston, ed., *Indiana Religious Intelligencer*, *1* (1828), 1.

65. Ibid., *1* (1829), 198–99.

66. Indianapolis, 9 April 1827, AHMS.

ignorant should fill the sacred office. . . . He who would be a profound student in the Bible,—a *workman that needeth not to be ashamed* should have a knowledge of the original languages in which the scriptures were written: for how shall he satisfy his own mind amid the clashing of sectarian views, unless he be able himself to go to the fountain head? Destitute of an acquaintance with the laws, customs, usages and sentiments of those nations where the Bible was written, how shall the minister employ in his service those rules of correct interpretation which are so essential in acquiring a critical knowledge of the scriptures? He whose great work is to combat the prejudices of men and mould the heart to the spirit of the gospel should be intimately acquainted with the laws of the mind. A thorough knowledge of mental philosophy will enable the minister "to touch skilfully the springs of thought" and to trace back and analyze the premises from which so many false inferences are deduced. No science affords such an extensive range for investigation as that of theology. It embraces almost every department of science and literature. And the more extensively acquainted with these various branches of knowledge the minister is, the more capable he is of comprehending the Bible. To enter even upon the threshold of theological science requires a vigorous mind, disciplined by habits of fixed attention.[67]

When seminaries were founded in the West to train ministers on the frontier, that did not markedly improve the rapport between most settlers and the educated preachers. John Finley Crowe came out from Princeton to begin the academy at Hanover. The first professor at Indiana Theological Seminary was John Matthews of Virginia. This rare

67. *A Discourse on Ministerial Qualifications* (Madison, 1831), p. 9.

man has been described by Edson in extravagant terms as able to define and trace everything through all its history to its ultimate sources, and able to pigeonhole facts so that they could be brought out at an instant to secure him quick success in any controversy. His learning was so incredibly organized, Edson claims, and his powers of definition so precise, that he rarely was overtopped. The Confession of Faith was his only textbook as a professor, and he began his courses with lectures on mental philosophy and logic. He used the Socratic method for both teaching and discussion.[68]

In contrast to this Virginian, there were two real Yankees, Caleb Mills and E. O. Hovey, who provided the leadership at Wabash College. They later fed students to Lane Seminary, which was heavy with eastern scholastic influence. Thus the home-grown preachers were not products of the frontier in the same sense that the Methodist or Baptist lay preachers were. They had simply relocated their books in a new and wilder land.

Presbyterian missionaries in Indiana were married men. Baynard Hall pointed out the hazards:

> Hence a New Purchase is not the most pleasant place in the world for boarding-school young ladies— or indeed for any females who have not muscles of oak and patience of an ox. Let then, no fair lady who can remain in an old settlement, venture into a new one from mere poetical reasons; or till she has long and deeply pondered this phrase and its cognates—"To work your own ash-hopper!" And if a nice young gentleman engaged to be married to a pretty deli- cate lily-flower of loveliness, is meditating "to flit" to a bran new settlement, let him know that out there rough men, with rare exceptions, regard wives as squaws, and as they often expressed their views to Mr. Carlton, "have no idee of sich weak, feminy, wimmin

68. *Contributions to Early History*, p. 245.

bodies as warnt brung up to sling a dinner-pot—kill
a varmint—and make leather britchises!"[69]

Yankee seminarians came with eastern wives and with their
debts for education still unpaid. It is remarkable that so few
echoes of wifely complaints appear in the reports. Mrs. Wheelock promptly sent back for New England schoolbooks and
opened a school in Greensburg designed to cure children and
their parents of "a heap of Kentuckyisms." Mrs. Chute put new
life into the "female prayer meeting" at Fort Wayne. Andover
student E. O. Hovey pondered carefully whether he should ask
a certain young lady to share missionary life with him. One
crucial factor was the liquidation of a $500 debt. This un-
doubtedly had a bearing on his decision to go to the West.[70]
The letters of Mrs. Hovey from the log cabin at Coal Creek,
and later from a faculty house at Wabash College, are history
in its more delightful form. Five western theologians did
"marry on the Range" by finding their wives among the
daughters in the manse of W. W. Martin. Consider the tribute
paid to Mrs. John Dickey:

> This wife shared his trials and successes for nearly
> thirty years and became the mother of eleven child-
> ren. The picture of the pioneer parsonage and its busy
> life would be sadly imperfect without the portrait of
> this Christian woman.
>
> She was worthy of her husband. Much of his use-
> fulness must be attributed to her. For the mainten-
> ance of the family she gave her full share of toil and
> self-denial, often living alone with her children for
> months together, disciplining them to industry and
> usefulness, while their father was absent upon long
> and laborious missionary journeys. She cultivated a
> garden which supplied many household wants.
> Reared as she had been on the frontier, her education

69. *New Purchase*, p. 264.
70. Andover Seminary, in a letter to Mrs. Charles White, Cazenovia, New
    York, 29 June 1831.

was at first limited, but under her husband's tuition she became a respectable scholar, able to instruct her own and her neighbors' children. She was an adept at the spinning-wheel and loom, and for many years made with her own hands all the linen and woolen cloth and garments for the family. There were also frequent additions to the exchequer from the sale of jeans of her manufacture. Such was her trust in God that fear never seemed to disturb her peace. She had lived for a time where the dread of prowling savages forbade the lighting of a lamp, or of a fire at night, and ordinary trouble produced no visible disturbance of her mind. In every good work she was foremost, whether it were making husk mattresses for the students at Hanover College, gathering supplies for destitute missionaries, or caring for the sick and unfortunate at home. The meagerness of her own household stores did not prevent her from doing much for others. In the absence of her husband the family altar was regularly maintained, and the Sabbath afternoon recitations from the Shorter Catechism were by no means omitted. Though her residence was on a farm and most of Mr. Dickey's public life was spent as pastor of a country church, she sustained a woman's weekly prayer-meeting. In the Sabbath-school and at public worship her place was seldom vacant, notwithstanding the claims of so large a family.[71]

The Reverend and Mrs. Samuel G. Lowry served as first pastor and wife at the Sand Creek Church in Decatur County. Thereafter the names Samuel and Almira appear so frequently on the baptismal rolls that one namesake observes that the people must have paid their preacher by naming their children after him.[72]

71. Edson, pp. 69–70. See also "A Memorial Address in Honor of Margaret Osborne Steele, Wife of Rev. John M. Dickey," delivered at Lexington, Indiana, 21 Nov. 1938, by Mrs. Albert G. Parker, Jr.

Sickness took its awful toll among the ministers and their families. Madison lost three ministers in rapid succession before calling the long-lived James H. Johnston in 1825. Perhaps the most able minister in the state, Benjamin C. Cressy, was killed by a "fever" in the very prime of life. Fall reports from the Wabash country repeatedly indicate that sickness was so prevalent that the ministers often could not preach and only small congregations could come to hear them if they did. In a very shaky hand William Woods wrote from Indianapolis: "Dear Brother, the reason of my not making my report at the proper time (Oct. 22) was owing to a severe attack of bilious fever from which I am now recovering. . . . But I will make you a full report for the year as soon as I am able to write."[73] Mary Hovey reported no less than eleven distinct cases of illness in her family within one 15-month period. Ague and fever were recurrent troubles, but the children also had severe cholic and measles, and Mr. Hovey endured a long sickness of his lungs. Yet Mrs. Hovey's attitude was one of thankfulness that their afflictions had been so light.[74] More grievous was the lot of James Wheelock at Clinton. In the fall of 1835 he reported that the whole family had been sick and that his oldest son had been taken. He, like so many others, had been attacked by the "bilious fever," and after days of fits and spasms he died. Soon Mr. Wheelock had to make the 130-mile trip to Salem for the synod. After suffering chills and fever all the way, he became so sick that within thirty miles of his destination he was obliged to turn back. By this time he was so weak that it took him two days on the road to reach Bloomington, the nearest town. [75] The next fall Wheelock had been in the East as an agent for Wabash College. He returned to find his three-year-old daughter and his six-year-old son dead, his wife at death's door, and the whole town sick. The boy had

72. *Seventy-Five Years: Anniversary Proceedings of the Founding of the Presbyterian Church, Kingston, Indiana, 18 December 1898* (Indianapolis, 1899), p. 9.
73. 17 Dec. 1835, AHMS.
74. In a letter to Mrs. Martha Carter, Oswego, New York, 27 April 1837.
75. 27 Oct. 1835, AHMS.

actually died from lack of nursing. But people in the country were afraid to come to town for fear of the "bilious fever" and in town it was impossible to get nurses or help of any kind. "What a sad wreck of my fond anticipations after six months absence. . . . I wish to be dumb before God and to walk softly all the rest of my appointed time on the earth. I hope He has chastised me in covenant faithfulness."[76]

Akin to the severe physical illnesses suffered by the missionaries was the stress of mental and emotional discouragement. Some of Indiana's early preachers from New England were never effective on the frontier. They were sincere young men overcome by a tough situation to which they could not adjust. Samuel Gregg of Ripley County reported that the people of Versailles knew very little except how to drink whiskey, and believed ultimately that all would be saved. Crossplains was no better. In fact, the coldness of his reception in the whole county would vie with that of any preacher on any spot of the globe where the Gospel was scorned. Anticipating the inevitable questions about why he had not set up temperance societies, Bible classes, and Sabbath schools, he bluntly stated that the materials of which to form such groups were simply not available. There were a few who professed religion in the county, but he felt certain that almost every one of them would have been excommunicated from an eastern church.[77] Daniel Jones found in Kosciusko County that the few Presbyterians there were all widely scattered, and that not even one of them showed any promise of helping him build up Zion. His daughter died; his family was sick; he himself got so weak he collapsed while preaching. Nobody seemed to care.[78] John Stocker concluded after a year at Delphi, "I have done my best to effect a change and have effected nothing or next to it, and I think some other man should try and let me go to some other field."[79]

76. Clinton, 4 Nov. 1836, AHMS.   77. 4 Sept. 1835, AHMS.
78. 25 April 1836, 26 April 1837, 14 Feb. 1838, 17 Aug. 1838: AHMS.
79. 9 Sept. 1836, AHMS.

On the other hand, born and bred Yankees like Leander Cobb, Benjamin C. Cressy, Ransom Hawley, E. O. Hovey, James H. Johnston, Solomon Kittredge, Caleb Mills, Martin M. Post, Isaac Reed, and Ashbel S. Wells did superb work in Indiana. They were able to disarm the prejudice against Presbyterians and to minister widely in the state. They formed the backbone of the New School Presbyterians.

Kentucky, Tennessee, and southern Ohio also furnished some effective preachers for Indiana. These preachers had come into Kentucky and Tennessee under the impetus of revival in the Valley of Virginia. They had come into Ohio as a continuation of back country Pennsylvania, especially through the agency of the Synod of Pittsburgh and the Western Missionary Society founded there in 1802. But in the early years in Indiana these sources of ministerial supply tended to trickle out. The Great Revival of Kentucky was not the kind of revival which produced a steady supply of Presbyterian ministers. In fact, the Great Revival did more to disquiet, discredit, and divide the Presbyterians than to prepare them to minister to a new state. Under sponsorship of the General Assembly and of Local Presbyterian bodies, some of these non-Yankee ministers traveled in Indiana. Some of them stayed. John Finley Crowe, William Martin, John Matthews, David Monfort, John Moreland, William Robinson, and Samuel Scott served long and honorably. They represent the heart of the Old School Presbyterians in the state, whose lot was made easier because the southern settlers of Indiana were often of the Scotch-Irish, old-side persuasion and were resentful of New England men.

In terms of endurance and usefulness, some of the pioneer preachers merit personal introduction here. William W. Martin (1781–1850) was a patriarch among Indiana preachers. Livonia was his home for twenty-four years, with only brief service elsewhere. At Livonia he operated his famous school and reared his ten children—the three boys to be ministers and five of the daughters to be wives of ministers. A manuscript sermon of Martin's, dating from the time of his licensure, shows him learned, careful, and rigid in doctrine. But contemporaries describe him as a sentimental orator capable of reducing his congregation or even the assembled Synod of Indiana to tears.[80] His prayer before sermon was generally forty-five minutes in length, and an irreverent son of John Dickey clocked one of Father Martin's prayers at one hour and thirty minutes. Livonia church was thriving in those days. The *Indiana Religious Intelligencer* for 9 January 1829 reported that Livonia had just added seventy-three members by profession of faith, and twenty-two by transfer.[81] There was a tavern for travelers at Livonia but most travelers, and certainly all Presbyterian preachers, stayed at William Martin's house. Baynard Hall and John Crozier record their pleasant impressions of this oasis in the wilderness.[82] Father Martin was of Scotch-Irish descent and of back country training; he did not understand or appreciate New England. So when the Old School–New School controversy warmed, he was capable of going into Bedford, holding a three-day meeting without consulting the session or the missionary pastor who had built up the church over seven years, and asking the congregation if they wanted to follow New School error or "remain Presbyterian" with him. The result was heartbreak and chaos.[83]

John McElroy Dickey (1789–1849) was the second resident minister in Indiana.[84] He was of Scotch-Irish descent, South Carolina born, and Kentucky trained. No mission society sent him; the people of Daviess County invited him and he came. "In May, 1815, still a licentiate under the care of Muhlenburg Presbytery he set out for his home in the wilderness with his wife and

80. Minnie B. Clark, "The Old Log College at Livonia," *IMH*, *23* (1927), 73–81.

81. *1*, 142–43.

82. Edson, p. 106. Hall, pp. 57–58.

83. Solomon Kittredge, Bedford, 12 Nov. 1839, AHMS.

84. Ezra H. Gillett, *History of the Presbyterian Church in the United States of America* (2 vols. Philadelphia, 1864), *2*, 397.

their infant daughter. The family and all their earthly goods were carried on the backs of two horses. His library consisted of a Bible, Buck's 'Theological Dictionary,' Bunyan's 'Pilgrim's Progress,' and Fisher's 'Catechisms.' When the ferriage across the Ohio was paid they had a single shilling left.''[85] The people could not be expected to support him fully, and he proved himself a useful citizen by farming, teaching a singing class, surveying, and teaching school. He wrote deeds, wills, and advertisements. With the help of neighbors he built his house and schoolhouse; the congregation built a meetinghouse. After four years Dickey moved to Scott County and was installed pastor of New Lexington and New Washington churches, the first formal installation in the state. There he labored twenty-eight years, until poor health forced retirement. Dickey was father of twelve children and sort of rural bishop of all southern Indiana. Always a friend of missions, he rode for the Assembly's Committee of Missions, for the Indiana Missionary Society, and for the American Home Missionary Society. He never missed a presbytery or synod meeting except those held just a few weeks before his death. By his own admission he was a poor agent when it came to making collections for missionary societies. In 1830 he went out as agent for the American Home Missionary Society because it was not convenient for Johnston to go. He toured twenty-five days, preached fifteen times, addressed three Sabbath schools, and traveled 428 miles. When he got back, all he had to submit was an expense account and a long list of places to which the American Home Missionary Society should send missionaries. He organized no associations auxiliary to the American Home Missionary Society on that trip, though he did scatter a few copies of the constitution; he collected no money. Absalom Peters, executive secretary for the Society, must have had to agree with Dickey when he judged himself a poor agent.[86] However, Dickey was a kind of perpetual missionary. His own

85. Edson, p. 65.
86. Clark County, 17 Aug. 1830, AHMS.

valuable *Brief History of the Presbyterian Church in Indiana* indicates that he organized six Presbyterian churches and encouraged many. Further, he was a missionary statesman—had his counsel been well taken it might have prevented the Old School–New School split in the West.

James H. Johnston (1798–1876) represents the city preacher in early Indiana. Madison was a metropolis in the forest, actually to be a rival of Cincinnati for the Ohio River pork-packing trade. It was to Madison that Johnston came in 1824 as a Yankee missionary of the United Domestic Missionary Society of New York. He had been a top scholar at Hamilton College and Princeton Seminary. The Madison Church needed a pastor and they called Johnston. The combination of his ability and prestige gave him a leading place in Presbyterian affairs. Within two years he became executive secretary of the Indiana Missionary Society; missionaries from the East reported to him for placement in Indiana.[87] He edited the *Indiana Religious Intelligencer*, a weekly missionary paper. When the Synod of Indiana convened for its first meeting in 1826, John M. Dickey was named moderator and James H. Johnston, then twenty-eight, was made clerk. He was repeatedly named as clerk and given major committee responsibility. Madison was one of the few places in Indiana not dealt a hard blow by the Old School–New School division. When the issue was agitated, the membership was large enough so that Johnston and his New School followers could build a new meetinghouse and form a new congregation without crippling the old church. After eighteen years Johnston left Madison to serve as pastor, teacher, and missionary in the Crawfordsville area. His letters as missionary, agent, and secretary to the American Home Missionary Society make a large file. They are marked by good spirit and good sense. He was one of Indiana's most useful pioneers.

Isaac Reed (1787–1858) is difficult to locate in Indiana

87. James H. Johnston, *A Ministry of Forty Years in Indiana* (Indianapolis, 1865), p. 9. See also Johnston, 13 June 1827, AHMS; Edson, p. 201.

because he was always on the move. Significantly, his valuable journal is entitled *The Christian Traveller*. As a licentiate of the Fairfield Congregational Association he came west for his health. After a bout with the western "bilious fever," he declared himself "greatly deceived respecting the climate," but subsequently he seems to have thrived on it. For a year, beginning in October 1818, he served as minister in New Albany, gathering the first Sabbath school in the state. Then he bought a farm of eighty acres in Owen County, proposing a simple and helpful plan. He would live in his "Cottage of Peace," serve as pastor of local Bethany church for one-half his time, and spend the other half traversing the state as missionary of an eastern society.[88] In 1824 he rode 2,480 miles in his missionary labors. Besides these travels he seems always to have been posting to New York, or Illinois, or Missouri lest some opportunity be overlooked. At least eight churches were organized by him, including Greencastle, Crawfordsville, Bloomington, and Greenwood.

Benjamin C. Cressy (died 1834) is the most winsome of the Yankee missionaries. He did all things well. After his first three months at Salem, he reported much house-to-house visitation, five well-organized Sabbath schools (with some 500 scholars) in his two congregations, new Sabbath-school books valued at eighty-five dollars, youth budget plan in the Sabbath schools, a Bible class of fifty members being used as teacher training for the Sabbath schools, regular prayer meetings including the "monthly concert" for missions, a missionary society, a tract society, contributions "to aid pious indigent youths preparing for the ministry," and a working plan to supply every destitute family in the county with a copy of the Scriptures within twelve months. This is all reported in artless

---

88. *Christian Traveller*, pp. 138–39. This is essentially the same plan recommended by Samuel G. Lowry to Absalom Peters, 19 Feb. 1835. Let each missionary have at least a small circuit. "Regular pastoral duties in smaller fields are the grand means of building up churches and strengthening the stakes; but we must do something also to *lengthen the cords*."

fashion without evidence of bragging. Cressy regretted that in these first three months he had not had time to do much for the promotion of temperance. He indicated, however, that he was at least preparing the way for an all-out campaign. Kittredge's address had already been circulated, and Beecher's sermons, having just arrived would soon follow.[89] The second quarter brought a revival, with thirty-seven added to the church. By the third quarter the number added had grown to fifty-four, and a county temperance society of 448 members had been organized.

> These benevolent efforts have called forth from those inimical to these proceedings a strength and virulence of opposition which I hope may not be witnessed in other places. "Church and state"; "down with the Presbyterians" is the popular cry. I rejoice Sir, that I belong to that hated denomination, who have conferred on them the abundant honour of "turning the world upside down" by their benevolent exertions to redeem man from the thraldom of sin. . . . If any have flattered themselves that the devil's kingdom in this Western land will be wrested from his grasp without a desperate struggle, they have been grandly mistaken.[90]

Cressy was a world mover. When he preached at sacramental meetings either revival came or at least "some mercy drops" fell. When Cressy went as agent for the American Home Missionary Society, the local subscriptions rose sharply. When Cressy delivered twelve lectures on the authenticity of the Bible, the place was crowded with people who were solemn and attentive.[91] To read his *Appeal in Behalf of Indiana Theological Seminary*[92] is to reach for a checkbook. On 10 July 1834 Cressy died of the "cholera morbus." The news traveled the frontier like a shock wave:

89. Cressy, 13 Sept. 1829, AHMS.
90. Ibid., 7 June 1830.
91. Ibid., 7 Jan 1834, 20 May 1834, 15 June 1832.
92. 16 pp.

The Rev. B. C. Cressy is no more . . . a recent event
of Divine Providence which has deeply afflicted the
friends of Zion in this vicinity and no doubt will be
felt very extensively in this country. It is a mysterious
providence to us. We cannot understand why a man
of preeminent usefulness in the bloom of life and
whose labors have so signally been blessed of God
should be so suddenly called away from us. But it is
all well—the Judge of all the earth has done right.[93]

James A. Carnahan (1802–1879) went from Father Martin's
"college" at Livonia to Auburn Seminary in New York. He
came back as a missionary of the American Home Missionary
Society in 1830, God's gift to the upper Wabash country.
Because the mission societies were sending out some preachers
and because the Wabash country received a few more Yankee
settlers, the Presbyterians made good progress there. James
Crawford, Martin Post, and James Carnahan were a mighty
trio in the newly settled north central portion of the state. At
the new settlement of Lafayette, Carnahan became the second
pastor of the Presbyterian Church and helped the congregation build their first edifice. He organized churches at West
Lafayette, Frankfort, Dayton, and Monticello. For four years
he was pastor at Delphi. Carnahan was a fine figure of a man
with marvelous endurance. He could ride all day on horseback
over bad roads in bad weather, and then preach the same night
with great vigor.[94] When eight men met at the site chosen for
Wabash College, six-foot, 220-pound Carnahan drove the
stake to mark the school's location; he was a trustee of the
college for forty-six years. After 1838 his home and his pastorate were at Dayton, Indiana, but his ministry included missionary service and pastoral labors over much of northern

93. Moody Chase, Orleans, 14 July 1834, AHMS.
94. *Indianapolis Sunday Star*, 20 Nov. 1932, quoting President Tuttle of
 Wabash College. This issue has a very good feature article by Bessie
 Lynn Hufford and a picture of Carnahan. See also *Hand Book of the
 Dayton Memorial Presbyterian Church, 1834–1934* (Dayton, 1934), pp. 4–9.

Indiana. He traveled and preached most extensively in summer and fall because his people were widely scattered; these seasons offered the best weather for riding and worshiping out-of-doors.[95] Carnahan had the vision of Zion. His report for 20 August 1835 takes time for a bit of prospect and retrospect:

> Whatever others may say, this valley of the Wabash has been made to sound with the praises of Almighty God through the instrumentality of this Society. Here have been churches planted; lights kindled up, and souls saved which shall shine to the glory of God the Father, Son and Holy Ghost forever and which shall be as stars in the crown of rejoicing of those who have lent their aid in the good cause. It would do your soul good to see the changes that have been wrought here since I first set my feet upon these beautiful plains. It is a matter which I contemplate with great delight. And especially when I carry my thought forward, and in imagination call up what is to be hereafter. I fancy the Sabbath has come and as far as the eye can see, I behold the teaming population with joyful steps hastening to the house of God there to offer up praise and prayers.[96]

Martin M. Post (1805–76) was born in Vermont and educated at Andover Seminary. A licentiate of the Andover Association and an ordinand of Londonderry Presbytery, he came to Indiana as a missionary of the American Home Missionary Society. On Christmas week he came to Logansport, a very new community of thirty or forty families, and here he stayed. The Presbyterian Church was the first on the scene, although only two persons in the area had ever been Presbyterian members. "I came here without experience in the duties of my calling, and with little practical knowledge of men, and none of Western life. Against strong withholding motives, induced decisively by a conviction of the superior claims of the

95. Carnahan, 3 July 1832, AHMS. 96. AHMS.

new States on any little service my life could render, I sought my way, alone, to Indiana in the autumn of 1829."[97] The woods were still full of Indians, regularly made drunk and fleeced by enterprising white men. Post promoted the range of good causes. He superintended the first Sabbath school in 1830, visited all families in the county to supply copies of the Bible in 1831, distributed tracts, established the first temperance society in 1831, and encouraged its growth to 250 members by 1837. For many years at least half of Post's ministry was out of town. Gradually these isolated settlers formed country congregations which, under his tireless encouragement, had built churches by 1860. He had frequently gone to Miamisport, which flourished until it merged with Peru. He went to Marion, to South Bend, LaPorte, Michigan City, Valparaiso, and many others.[98] As he explored, Post sent letters to the American Home Missionary Society urging the importance of locations like Michigan City and the claims of the whole Wabash country. Canals, state roads, and the natural fertility were bound to make this an important area. He reported that there was not a handful of Presbyterians in most of these places, but that the citizens in general would support a minister if one came. For a bit of added motivation: "The Lord's Supper was administered here on the last Sabbath . . . We were seriously interrupted in the morning by the Roman Catholics. They took possession of the house of worship at an early hour and retained it till some time in the afternoon in the celebration of mass interspersed with declamations against Protestants and in glorification of the 'Holy Mother.'" By 1837 Post could send along some welcome news. After seven years of service he had been officially installed as pastor at Logansport, and he joyfully reported that his congregation felt it to be both their duty and their privilege to provide for their pastor's support.[99]

97. *A Retrospect after Thirty Years' Ministry at Logansport, Indiana* (Logansport, 1860), p. 8. 98. Ibid., p. 19.
99. 1 Oct. 1834, 3 July 1834, 26 June 1833, 29 March 1832, 24 May 1830, 17 June 1837: AHMS.

James Chute (1788–1835) was the pioneer preacher at Fort Wayne. He was the son of a Massachusetts farmer, educated in New England schools and Dartmouth College. He moved west to teach at Pittsburgh and then at Cincinnati. While in Cincinnati he studied theology with Joshua L. Wilson and was licensed to preach. It was eighteen years after his graduation from college that he moved to Fort Wayne. The American Home Missionary Society counted Fort Wayne a strategic spot and therefore commissioned him as a missionary. Chute appears to have been a zealous but only fairly successful worker. Fort Wayne was a tough place. Much of the population was composed of Indians, traders, speculators, and canal laborers. Chute preached to everybody in the county who would hear him, including the men on the canal. He preached in all the neighborhoods for the sake of those not accustomed to inconveniencing themselves by traveling to meetings. He pushed the temperance cause by law and persuasion until the sale of liquor to Indians was prohibited, the issue of whiskey as standard provision to canal workers was halted, and the temperance society gained ground to the point that consumption of whiskey dropped to one-eighth of what it had been two years earlier. When eighty people died in a single quarter, he ministered faithfully among the sick.

Still the church grew very slowly. Chute kept explaining why the cost of living was so high and applying for more mission aid. Besides serving his seven regular preaching points in his home county, he was always pleading the cause of his neighbors to the American Home Missionary Society. Huntington, Wabash, and Peru were among the county towns he worried about. He reported that at Huntington especially there were people who were eager for preaching. These people had asked him to come as often as possible to visit them.[100] Construction of a church building was finally begun in 1835, but Chute did not live to occupy its

100. 13 Jan. 1835, 8 July 1835, 25 Sept. 1834, 28 June 1834, 12 Sept. 1833, 12 Sept. 1832, 13 June 1832, 12 March 1832, 12 Dec. 1831: AHMS.

pulpit. He died that year of "bilious fever."[101]

The aim of the main body of Presbyterian preachers may not have been entirely at one with the aims of the settlers, especially the southern ones. Their goal was that every village should have a settled and educated ministry to build up Zion. They were unrelenting "do-gooders" in a generation and place which sorely needed them but was of little mind to support them. Considering the limitations of the preachers' forces and the obstacles to be overcome, they can be called nothing less than heroic:

> Did I not regard this as an important post to be occupied by the means of grace, I should not feel it my duty to stay here another month. The church is small and scattered over a large territory, so that it is impossible to bring them to feel and act together. They are generally in low circumstances as it respects this world; just struggling to open their farms and pay their debts. Besides this, the community is divided into so may religious sects (not less than eight) and some of these so utterly opposed to evangelical truth, that it causes the faith of the missionary sometimes almost to fail him that he will ever see truth triumph over error. Infidelity too has a strong hold here. These and some other things are discouraging. But there are some things of a more cheering character. This is certainly an important field of labor. Bedford is a growing place in the midst of a rich country of land. Our little church the past year has had an accession of nine members. And we trust that God has shed down a few mercy drops upon this dry and thirsty hill of Zion. And we still hope that mercy is in store for this people, and that this moral wilderness will yet bud and blossom as the rose.[102]

101. *In Memoriam: Rev. James Chute, First Pastor of the First Presbyterian Church of Fort Wayne* (Fort Wayne, 1874), p. 4.
102. Solomon Kittredge, Bedford, 10 April 1835, AHMS.

Vincennes congregation was the first Presbyterian church in Indiana, Charlestown's was the second, and Washington's was the third. Presbyterians gathered for worship in Indiana from about 1800. Transylvania Presbytery named supply preachers north of the Ohio beginning in 1803.

In 1806 the "church of Indiana" was organized in the barn of Colonel Small, about two miles east of Vincennes.[1] By 1828 John Dickey could list forty-five churches in Indiana and add that the number was probably closer to fifty, because there were several churches in the eastern part of the state under the care of the Presbyteries of Cincinnati and Miami.[2]

Vincennes, Charlestown, Madison, New Albany, and Indianapolis are examples of early churches located at important population centers. A host of others were founded on good hopes of serving population centers and on the zeal of missionaries to raise up Zion in every community where a nucleus of the faithful could be organized. It does not follow, however, that the earliest churches or the largest towns were most effective in raising up new Presbyterian congregations. Madison

1. Edson, *Contributions to Early History*, p. 41.
2. *Brief History*, pp. 10–11.

took leadership in missionary work because James H. Johnston was there. But Corydon church, constituted at the state capital in 1819, had only seven members at the beginning and remained destitute until 1824. Vincennes had three church houses as part of the "Indiana Church," but all three congregations together could not support a minister in 1830 without considerable help from the American Home Missionary Society.[3] On the other hand, the country points of New Lexington and New Washington contracted for two-thirds of the time of John M. Dickey. With the remaining third, this country pastor organized and cared for a vast missionary parish. Columbus church is a case in point. The history of that church says of Dickey:

> His labor here dates from the time when only one or two log cabins had been built at this point, and a few families had settled here and there in this region. He frequently passed this way journeying from Madison along trails blazed through the woods. When as the fruit of his labor an organized congregation was formed, he continued for many years to give it his tender care, and at one time supplied it for six months one Sabbath each month. Every year he held meetings that continued several days, baptizing children, receiving new members to the church, and administering communion. It is recorded that he preached here as late as 1842.[4]

There was nothing automatic about the establishment of Presbyterian churches in Indiana. It depended upon deliberate "missionating" as the preachers called it. Sometimes this was done well, sometimes very poorly.

Ingenuity was the order of the day in providing meeting

3. Samuel Alexander, Vincennes, 18 Aug. 1828, 24 Nov. 1829, 12 Jan. 1830, 20 April 1830: AHMS.
4. From the historical sketch printed in the *Program for Centennial Week of the Presbyterian Church, Columbus, Indiana, 1824–1924.*

places for those early congregations. The best available was none too good. Eastern sources for building funds were few. Calvin Butler did two months of "the most laborious, perplexing service" soliciting money in the East for the meetinghouse in Evansville but obtained only $320. In March 1831 Butler appealed to the American Home Missionary Society for aid. Evansville had been settled fourteen years and still had no house of worship for any denomination. Lately there had come reports of a grant of $1,000 available to any church which would admit to membership only those persons who pledged total abstinence from alcoholic drinks. Butler said that his Evansville congregation had required abstinence from the beginning, before they heard of any financial benefits, but if any grant was to be made on that basis, they certainly needed the money for their new building.[5]

One obvious solution to the shortage of meetinghouses was to meet outdoors in the woods. The first resident Presbyterian preacher in the state, Samuel T. Scott, used such a "sequestered sylvan sanctuary,"[6] consisting of a rough platform and a great number of rustic benches. Even the session meetings of the Indiana Church were held here prior to 1815. Eastern missionaries wrote back home that their church included a membership scattered over a county. Among the half dozen preaching points of the congregation would be a "grove." In fact, almost every community maintained a grove to which the congregation adjourned for occasions involving large crowds— revivals or sacramental occasions. Salem Presbytery met in Charlestown in October 1830 and made a formal resolve that, considering the state of the population and its character, a missionary effort was urgently needed, and since grove meetings which lasted several days seemed to encourage such efforts, they should be held regularly.[7]

Even more usual was the procedure of holding worship services in cabins at various points of the parish. Thus the New

5. 28 March 1831, 2 Dec. 1831: AHMS.
6. Edson, p. 43.   7. MSP, *1*, 84–85.

Providence church was organized in the Wishard cabin near Indianapolis, and the Greenwood church was organized in the Smock cabin. J. D. Connor of Wabash generalized that the church beginnings were all alike: first the worship was conducted in members' cabins; then a room was rented where services could be held; later a subscription paper was circulated and signed; and finally a meetinghouse was built and furnished.[8] The cabin meetings were often a real adventure. In one case the pulpit was a chair and the preacher stood behind it. If he should get emphatic and thump the pulpit on the floor, all the geese, pigs, and dogs under the house would answer in chorus. Meetings were subject to interruption at any time when a neighbor burst in with the universal greeting, "Well, who keeps house?"[9] J. W. Blythe tells of cabin preaching during his missionary tour in northern Indiana as an appointee of the General Assembly's Board in 1832:

> I would be directed from one neighborhood to another and told to inquire for such or such a man— usually an elder from Kentucky or somewhere else. At his house I would take up somewhere during the afternoon. Upon alighting the first question asked would be Ar'n't you a Preacher—The second was sure to follow— Will you preach tonight. And while a supper was gotten for me and the faithful horse cared for, notice was given. This notice was generally by blast of horn. They all knew by the number of blasts that it meant preaching and by previous arrangement when it was to be held. I would have from twenty to fifty hearers. It was not a sermon if it occupied less than an hour in delivering.
>
> It was a uniform custom, broken with few exceptions, for every man to carry his hat upon his head— even after he entered the house. But as soon as I rose

8. *A Centennial History of the Presbyterian Church of Wabash, Indiana, 1836–1936*, p. 35.
9. Hall, *New Purchase*, pp. 170–75, 67.

for the service, every hat was placed upon the floor beside and within reach of the owner's hand. And thus they sat while listening to God's Word, even though that word was spoken by an almost beardless boy. It marked the reverence of those uncultivated men for this Word. Before it they would sit or stand uncovered and before nothing else.

As soon as the service was at an end they seemed to feel the want of a covering for their heads to assure them ease in social intercourse. So every one took naturally to his hat and he was himself again. Then perhaps the oldest man among them, or the man to whom they were in the habit of looking up for direction, would turn to me with the question, "Well Stranger what is the news from the settlements." More generally, "What is the news from Kentucky."[10]

As soon as the country was built up enough to have public buildings, these would be available for Presbyterian services in turn. The public building would often be used for the courthouse, the schoolhouse, all elections, the meetings of societies and religious denominations and for meetings of any public purpose. Many of these buildings were inconvenient and uncomfortable especially in winter. More than one church group suffered from the lack of a house of worship, but most of them did not have the means to build one. Jeremiah R. Barnes put his finger on the difficulty of having so many preachers of several different denominations supplying the people that no single minister ever had sufficient opportunity to reach them deeply enough to do permanent good. The result was that these Christians gradually began to lose their sense of responsibility.[11] At Rising Sun in 1831 the Presbyterians were meeting in the Methodist house of worship. At Fort Wayne in the same year, the Presbyterians and the Methodists shared use of the "Free

10. Handwritten statement respecting his first visit to the bounds of the Indiana Synod, 1832.
11. Evansville, 24 March 1837, AHMS.

Mason Hall."[12] Everywhere the Presbyterians wanted their own houses of worship. An agent for the American Home Missionary Society reported that the lack of churches was more responsible than any other factor for the loss of Christians in Indiana.[13] The Presbytery of Salem affirmed that good spirit with other denominations was highly desirable but building a union church was not the way to achieve it. They advocated that strictly Presbyterian meetinghouses be erected.[14]

Building a meetinghouse took a lot of doing. Even choosing the location was no small matter. Members in the country were not at all convinced that the matter was solved by locating in the county seat. Happy was the church whose minister combined the talents of pastor and master carpenter. John Stocker, "an eastern man," came to Delphi in November 1835 and demonstrated how not to get a church built. He made a very firm pronouncement to the effect that construction of a meetinghouse was of the utmost importance; consequently, if it were not built within what he deemed to be a reasonable length of time, he could not possibly remain pastor. A society was organized and the trustees were urged to proceed without delay. But after a lot was purchased nothing more was done.[15] Stocker left town. On the other hand, Benjamin M. Nyce of Columbus is given complete credit for erection of the first Presbyterian meetinghouse there. He solicited money, bought material, and wielded the hammer in construction. When offered a load of lumber, he went personally with the largest team and wagon at hand.[16] Rushville church began a building program by commissioning pastor D. M. Stewart to make the brick and to get the materials for the new building.[17] In 1836

12. William Lewis, Rising Sun, 14 Nov. 1831; James Chute, Fort Wayne, 12 Dec. 1831: AHMS.
13. James Thomson, Crawfordsville, 10 June 1834, AHMS.
14. MSP, 2, 50.   15. 9 September 1836, AHMS.
16. From the historical sketch printed in the Columbus church *Centennial Program*.
17. *Centennial of the Organization of the First Presbyterian Church, Rushville, Indiana, 1825–1925*.

Kingston church contracted for construction of a brick church building. On an appointed day the trustees and bidders assembled. A trustee mounted the block and cried the bids, auction fashion, while the contractors competed, bidding downward.[18] In the nineteenth-century life story of most congregations there was a period of meeting in homes and public buildings, a homely church structure, a larger and finer building within twenty years, a fire or accidental loss, and finally a building of brick or stone having some pretension to elegance. Even to such a rough pattern there are many exceptions. In Indianapolis a building valued at $1,600 was provided before the church was formed,[19] and in Huntington the first Presbyterian building constructed was a brick colonial valued at $4,000. Here the first pipe organ in the city was installed.[20]

Presbyterians who were fortunate enough to have a pastor at all generally had to be satisfied with one service of worship on Sunday. The minister had to move on to conduct service at another preaching point. But the sermon would be ample—at least an hour. Usually it would be either read or presented from copious notes, although E. O. Hovey wrote that his sermons were all extemporaneous and much longer than those written by the young New England ministers, and Thomas Cleland, the first recorded Presbyterian minister in Indiana, was a famous and moving extemporaneous speaker. In 1841 the General Assembly urged that reading sermons and using notes should be avoided.[21] Indianapolis Presbytery (Old School) agreed. But when the presbytery followed up their injunction with an inquiry the next year, it was found that the recommendation had been disregarded. Ironically, only a short time before, this very presbytery had held up the ordination of Colin McKinney because his sermon before the presby-

18. Kingston church, *Seventy-Five Years*, p. 15.
19. Julia M. Moores, "Early Times in Indianapolis." *IMH, 8* (1912), 136.
20. *Centennial Celebration of the First Presbyterian Church, Huntington, Indiana, 1843–1943*, p. 6.
21. "Minutes," p. 448.

tery was not satisfactory, having been partly extemporane-
ous.[22] Most of the sermons, however, were probably written or
at least showed the marks of careful scholastic preparation.
Perennial sermon subjects included Prayer, Perseverance of
the Saints, Sanctification of the Sabbath, Resurrection, Temperance, Predestination, Baptism, Repentance, Judgment,
Means of Grace, Way of Salvation, Religious Instruction of
Children, Scriptural Conditions of Church Membership,
Heretical Doctrines, Support of the Ministry, Atonement,
Human Ability.[23] The presbytery required that some of these
topics be presented to the congregations. One brother even
called the attention of his presbytery to the great obligation
which the church and the world owed to the labors of the
Westminster Assembly for their important exertions in behalf
of sound doctrine, civil liberty, and religious liberty. He moved
that the last Sabbath in December be set apart as a day of
special instruction on this subject. The motion was carried.[24]

Hymns were "lined out" for the congregation in the early
days—that is, the minister or song leader would read out two
lines of the hymn, which the congregation would sing, and so
on to the end of the hymn. The repertory was small. One song
leader went East and learned the tune "Boylston." Back in
Indianapolis he showed his admiration for the new tune by
raising it five times in one Sunday.[25] By 1846 Indianapolis
Presbytery (Old School) had recommended the Assembly's
new collection of psalms and hymns for all churches and
homes.[26] This marked the end of an era in which every congregation had made its choice whether to sing the psalms of
Rous or of Watts. Now they were ready to go beyond the singing of psalms. In spite of the grumbling of Scotch-Irish elders
about "worshiping God with a mere machine," pianos and
organs became acceptable by 1850.

22. MIP, OS, *1*, 118, 83.
23. This list is gleaned from the "set sermons" of Indianapolis Presbytery,
Old School, 1837–1845.   25. Moores, "Early Times," *IMH, 8,* 138.
24. MLP, *1*, 2–3.   26. MIP, OS, *1*, 262.

Sunday worship service was not the sum of church activity by any means. In fact there was to be a regular meeting every Sunday even if there was no minister present. There was the Sabbath school with its recitations and its library, to be supplemented with Bible study classes for adults, on either a week night or Sunday, the subject matter preferably coordinated with the lessons of the young people. There was the weekly prayer meeting and the monthly "concert of prayer" for missions. The church might well have an auxiliary temperance society, tract society, Bible society, or education society, with regular meetings. There were beginnings of organized women's work: "We have recently formed a maternal association and sewing society which promises good and we have the pleasing prospect of being able in the course of the year to contribute something to the American Home Missionary Society."[27] Missionary Ashbel Wells at New Albany reported that the Female Bible Society of his church would soon complete the work of supplying every destitute family in the county with the word of God.[28] They did it—probably the first county so supplied in the state. The Greencastle Presbyterian Church women were successively the Female Aid Society, Soldiers Aid Society, Willing Workers, Hatchet Sisters, and Ladies Aid.[29] Twice a year there was to be a special public service of catechizing the children and encouraging proper church and family relations.[30] Then there were regular meetings of the church officers. Besides all the bona fide church activities, wherever the congregation had a meetinghouse it was used for "reformers," debating clubs, political harangues, and all kinds of entertainment.[31] Even at worship service, the attendance at most early Presbyterian churches seems to have been about double the membership. A report that indicates this was not the result of a "preachers count" was made by three elders

27. Peter Crocker, Richmond, 15 Jan. 1838, AHMS.
28. 18 Nov. 1828, 5 Jan. 1830. AHMS.
29. *Centennial of the Presbyterian Church, Greencastle, Indiana* (1925), p. 8.
30. MMP, *1*, 62-4. MIP, *1*, 257.   31. *Seventy-Five Years*, p. 18.

from Lima in LaGrange County. They wrote that their church consisted of thirty-eight members, twenty-six of whom were women, and that they had two central meeting places, in each of which the congregation averaged about seventy-five persons.[32] The percentage of young people seems to have been about as varied as in modern churches. Solomon Kittredge packed the house with young people:

> My congregation in Bedford the past winter has been larger than usual. There are some things which make my Bedford congregation peculiarly interesting, and which give me great encouragement. In the first place, it is composed principally of young persons. I have been delighted frequently in entering my congregation to behold a large assembly, almost without exception, in the prime of life. My congregation has sometimes numbered over three hundred and perhaps not twenty of them over 35 years old. I have preached several times the past winter, exclusively to youth. On these occasions our house where we worshipped has been crowded to overflowing and many went away for want of room to get even within the entry. We then felt the need of a meeting house.[33]

Most important of all were the sacramental occasions. They were held as often as quarterly in the thriving congregations with a pastor. And the sacrament was an integral part of a revival or a meeting of the presbytery or synod. Rarely did a minister plan to lead such a service alone; he called in at least one neighboring preacher to assist. Communion services began on Friday, often a fast day, and continued through Monday.

At the communion service itself, the elements were customarily given at long, specially prepared communion tables. Thomas Cleland, as early as 1823 in Kentucky, had introduced the system of distributing the elements to communicants in the

32. Haven Cary, Oren Howard, and Henry Averin, 29 Oct. 1835: AHMS.
33. 31 March 1836, AHMS.

pews, but this innovation made little impression north of the Ohio. Isaac Reed described the classic procedure:

> As the Presbyterians there are chiefly from the southern states, they have brought with them the customs of the Presbyterians of Virginia and Carolina; and these have brought them from the mother church in Scotland. One of these customs is, to have a sacramental meeting consist of several successive days, including a Sabbath. At this meeting it is common to have a plurality of ministers. It is in this way that the ministers keep up a system of exchange. You assist me, and I assist you in return. The meeting begins either Friday or Saturday, and closes Monday;— Sabbath is the communion. Preaching each day is at the same place, which is either a meeting-house, or a stand in some piece of woods; and often where there is a meeting-house, the house is so small, and the assembly so large, that they have to go to the woods. The congregation consists of the people of the congregation, where the meeting is held, and numbers, from others round about. One or two sermons is preached each day, and frequently some at night in neighbourhoods. On the Sabbath a sermon is preached before communion, called "the action sermon." Then the other minister rises and introduces the communion service according to the Directory. He then gives out the institutional hymn; and as they are singing that, the ministers go to the table, and as many communicants as can sit on each side of it. The table is a long one. The minister who preached the sermon, sits at the table; and the other gives thanks and breaks and gives out the bread, and the cup. The ruling elders serve at the table. When all have received, another hymn is sung; and while singing, these withdraw, and the table fills again. Then the other minister serves,

and the first communes. In like manner, if there are more ministers, and if there are more tables, till all are served. I have sometimes seen five settings: I have myself served at three, when no other minister was with me. Monday they assemble early, and dismiss about mid-day. This practice leads the Christians to know and love one another, all round a large tract of country, and cherishes this spirit and practice of hospitality. When in missionary service, I have held sacramental meetings; I have sometimes seen members from six different Presbyterian churches, and all destitute. Some of these came 25, and others 30 miles, purposely to attend the meeting. In some cases, I have seen women who walked 10 miles, to be at such a meeting.[34]

The hospitality of ministers and church members in these extended sacramental meetings was remarkable. One member of John M. Dickey's family recalled his mixed reactions to these gatherings. He enjoyed the good cheer, the singing, and the social events but dreaded having to sleep on the bare floor without even a pillow in order that the visitors might have beds and covers. He remembered that one of his neighbors was said to have room for sixty guests, while the young men and the boys slept on hay in the barns. Despite the added work that so much company demanded of the women, things were always arranged so that they could attend the public meetings.[35] During these days there was preaching morning, noon, and night. Ludwig David von Schweinitz, a Moravian bishop, in 1831 recorded his impressions of these proceedings as an outsider. He was delayed in Madison and on Friday morning was promptly escorted to Johnston's church, where a four-day meeting was just beginning:

> Such "meetings" are held everywhere to produce revivals and were continued daily during our entire

34. *Christian Traveller*, pp. 228–30.   35. Edson, p. 70.

stay here without interruption, save for meals and short intermissions, from nine o'clock in the morning until after eleven o'clock at night. After a very brief address several members of the church were asked to offer prayer, and hymns were sung in the intermission. Sometimes, also, members of the congregation were asked to sing a hymn, which they did, but it was always the same, "Alas! and did my Savior bleed." Then the various ministers present likewise offered long prayers, sang hymns, and delivered very eloquent sermons. After the first prayer meeting, at which, among others, a venerable old man offered a touching evangelical prayer in simple, heartfelt language—which unfortunately he repeated just the same way every day—Mr. Hendricks introduced me to Mr. Johnston, the Presbyterian minister here.

Von Schweinitz felt himself in a fearful dilemma on Sunday afternoon of that Madison meeting. The Lord's Supper was celebrated and all Christians were issued a solemn invitation to partake, regardless of denomination. The whole town knew he was a minister and he did not want to hesitate. Yet the occasion was so foreign to him that he could not bring himself to commune.

From Sunday on, when those in whom the Spirit was manifest, were repeatedly asked to come forward in public, the prayers and discourses were most eagerly directed at producing expressions of revival. Some young women had finally stepped up in the evening and were worked upon, in public and in private, with indescribable zeal. During the whole time the church was crowded.

On Monday, the 30th, without any noticeable interference with the meeting, a very large muster of militia was held, at which a number of candidates at the impending elections for Congress, state governor, and Assembly, made speeches to the people and great excesses were committed. Although no drinks at all were served in respectable inns, I have rarely seen so many people drunk and nowhere so many brawls and rows, for the populace of Indiana develops a fearful rudeness on such occasions.[36]

Presbyterians intended their sacramental occasions to be emotionally moving. "Manifestations" were welcome. They desired strong conviction and even tears, but no "disorder." When John Ross of Wayne County was preaching in the home of Mr. Ahearts near Greenville, at the singing of the last hymn Mrs. Ahearts fell on her knees and cried out, "O do pray for me, a poor and miserable sinner." Ross reported that she sobbed violently and wept, but fearing that some disorder might develop he chose to continue the worship service. At the end of the singing she fainted, but after being given a little water she revived and was helped to her room. Ross conferred with her later and at the next communion she was received on profession of faith, over the violent protest of her husband. The husband was so violently opposed, in fact, that the sight of a Bible or hymnbook sent him into a rage. He made it plain that his wife must leave the Presbyterian Church or leave him. But she stayed with both, apparently at some risk of life and limb.[37]

At these sacramental services members were added to the churches. A host of accounts indicates a three-step procedure in admission to church membership. First there had to be conviction of sin and anxiety concerning the state of the soul: "many are anxious crying 'what must we do to be saved?'" The use of "anxious seats" was common. Then came a degree of assurance: "some entertain a hope of having passed from death unto life," followed by examination by the session (governing elders) and admission to the Lord's Supper. Very

36. L. D. von Schweinitz, *The Journey of Lewis David von Schweinitz to Goshen, Bartholomew County in 1831*, trans. Adolf Gerber, IHSP, 8 (Indianapolis, 1927), 227–30.
37. 28 Sept. 1830, 21 Dec. 1830: AHMS.

rarely did one person take all three steps at a single meeting or sacramental occasion. Ministers and elders were bidden to exercise great caution lest members be hastily received. At its third meeting at Vincennes in 1828, the Indiana Synod delivered itself at length on the subject of receiving church members, namely that extreme caution should be taken in their reception. The synod stated that candidates' names should be published for several weeks and that the elders should talk with the candidates frequently. This was to prevent admitting any "who prove only a dead weight, if not real enemies, to the church, and stumbling blocks to others."[38] Reports of pastors express the same concern. P. S. Cleland of Jeffersonville claimed he had no occasion to urge people to come into the church. Indeed, he said it was difficult to keep them out and his officers had to exercise great discretion in the admission of members.[39] This was a lesson the early Presbyterians seemed to have learned well. Invitation was not to church membership but to the "anxious seats." The proportion seems always to have been many anxious, some hopeful, and few or none received. There were exceptions. New Albany went off the list of mission churches with a flourish in 1830. Ashbel Wells reported in that year that the church had experienced a series of eventful four-day communion services. At the first of these, fifteen or twenty had come forward to the anxious seat asking the prayers of the church. Then a meeting in the grove had stirred the whole town, and over a hundred expressed anxiety and solemnity. The membership of the church was so strengthened that now they could turn from receiving aid to giving aid to others.[40]

Careful preparation for communion was taken for granted. Isaac Reed was not known as a stickler for rules, but when he came to Terre Haute on Saturday, 6 May 1826, he expected to preach at noon, preparatory to the Lord's Supper on the next

38. MIS, *1*, 46–49.
39. 2 July 1838, AHMS. See also *Indiana Religious Intelligencer*, *1* (1828), 86, 89.
40. 16 Nov. 1830, AHMS.

day. When no congregation assembled, the obvious conclusion was that the sacrament would not be administered next day. There is no hint of bitterness in the report in his journal. Reed preached on that Saturday night in the courthouse and on Sunday to "a large congregation." He remarked on the improved order of the town. But there was no communion service that weekend, since there had been no prior service of preparation.[41]

Yet there appears to have been no effort to ensure that only the ones who attended preparatory services should participate in the sacrament. John Stocker reported that he and Mr. Hummer of Lafayette conducted a sacramental meeting at Monticello, where a church of twenty-eight members had been organized. On Saturday night the usual preparatory service was held for the members, but on Sunday, which was the first Sabbath that preaching had ever been heard in that town, several hundred people gathered and about forty took communion. Methodists and Baptists joined with the Presbyterians in the Lord's Supper celebrated there in the wilderness. Stocker wrote that this was a precious and solemn occasion.[42] Communion tokens were not generally used in Indiana except among the highly conservative Presbyterian branches, the "Seeders" and "Covenanters."[43]

In the Presbyterian system of government, the local church is governed by its elected representatives, the elders. The elders, together with the minister, comprise the session. This body is

41. *Christian Traveller*, p. 182.
42. Delphi, 9 May 1836, AHMS.
43. These bits of wood or metal were sometimes issued at preparatory service on Friday or Saturday and required of all who wished to partake of the sacramental elements on Sunday. For a study of certain "psalm-singing" Presbyterians in Princeton, Indiana, see James A. Woodburn, *Scotch-Irish Presbyterians in Monroe County, Indiana*, IHSP, 4 (Indianapolis 1910), 437–522. See also Robert A. Woods, "Presbyterianism in Princeton, Indiana, from 1810 to 1930," *IMH*, 26 (1930), 93–125. Princeton had eleven denominations of Presbyterians before she exceeded a population of 2,500.

responsible for oversight of the total program of the local church and for proper counsel or care of the congregation. Elected elder delegates from the sessions and all the ministers in a given area make up the presbytery, a sort of corporate bishop. The presbytery examines and ordains candidates for the ministry; it exercises administrative, legislative, and judicial oversight of the churches in its bounds. Reception, installation, or dismissal of ministers is a presbytery function.

The synod embraces all presbyteries within its geographical bounds. In early Indiana the membership of the synod was simply the combined membership of its presbyteries. The synod exercises administrative and judicial oversight of the presbyteries and provides a channel of cooperation in support of educational or benevolent institutions and in planning of church programs. Decisions of the presbyteries may be appealed to the synod. But the presbyteries cannot be said to be entirely subject to the synod; the presbytery is the fundamental unit of Presbyterian government, the real seat of authority.[44] The synod reviews but does not actually control because certain rights are reserved to the presbyteries.

The General Assembly is composed of elected commissioners from the presbyteries, an equal number of elders and ministers being commissioned. This is the highest body of the Presbyterian Church, exercising administrative, legislative, and judicial oversight except as certain powers are constitutionally reserved to presbyteries. The Assembly has generally met once each year, except that from 1840 to 1849 the Presbyterian Church, New School, tried a plan which made the synods the final courts of appeal and held triennial Assemblies.[45]

Ideally, this form of government provides good flexibility for extension, even for following a frontier. The presbyteries on

44. This principle of the basic authority of the presbytery was affirmed in American Presbyterianism after sharp contention. See Leonard J. Trinterud, *The Forming of an American Tradition; A Re-examination of Colonial Presbyterianism* (Philadelphia, Westminster, 1949), pp. 81, 98, 328.
45. Drury, *Presbyterian Panorama*, p. 107. MIS, *1*, 267–69, 281.

the line of settlement kept their western boundaries open. As settlers poured in, synods constituted new presbyteries, and the General Assembly grouped the presbyteries into new synods. In general the system worked well.

From 1800 to 1830 the Presbyterian Church in the United States grew in membership from 20,000 to 173,000 and was regarded by some as the most influential church in America.[46] Everywhere it filled the frontiers with new presbyteries and synods. In Indiana it was the Transylvania, Washington, and Louisville Presbyteries of Kentucky and the Miami Presbytery of Ohio which first included the new settlements. The Salem (1824), Wabash (1825), and Madison (1825), Presbyteries were formed to become part of the new Synod of Indiana in 1826. As settlement proceeded to the north, Crawfordsville (1829), Indianapolis (1830), St. Joseph (1833), and Logansport (1835) Presbyteries were added to the Indiana synod. The Old School –New School division so confounded matters, however, that by 1851 fifteen presbyteries and four synods had been constituted with part or the whole of their jurisdiction within the state.

All this may look impressive on a map; but, in fact, wherever the main population stream was from the southern back country, the Presbyterian structure was often little more than a shell. Even small gains were enough to delight the hearts of Dickey and Johnston:

> Twenty-one years ago, I saw what was a "new thing" in Indiana, and that was 3 Presbyterian preachers together, and one of them not a resident of the state; two years afterwards I saw another new thing, and that was 4 Presbyterian preachers together, and one of them did not reside in the state. Now we have upwards of 60, more or less engaged in promoting the cause of the Redeemer and the salvation of souls; and other parts of the great West are equally supplied with the ministers of the gospel. Have we not abun-

46. George W. Allison, *Forest, Fort, and Faith: Historical Sketches of the Presbytery of Fort Wayne, Organized January 2, 1845* (1945), p. 9.

dant reasons for devout gratitude to God for what he has done for us?[47]

Missionary effort from the Assembly and the eastern societies helped somewhat to fill in the area with ministers and churches. Wherever a considerable city arose to supply a cosmopolitan constituency or wherever the population came from the East directly without a generation or more in the woods, things were likely to be easier. But in most of early Indiana there were not enough Presbyterian churches to allow a presbytery to function well. Add to this the fact that some missionaries behaved as foreign agents, thus taking little share in the presbytery and being little inclined to be "subject to their brethren in the Lord." Internal divisions leading up to the Old School–New School split only made matters worse. From one-third to one-half of the churches did not have a pastor. Presbyteries and synods were forever trying to decide about proper representation of pastorless churches in the church courts. Whatever the decision, the vacant churches rarely sent delegates unless an ecclesiastical fight was in prospect. A system of government which hinges upon a trained and responsible eldership had few trained elders in its membership, and a local church often numbered only a handful of men as communicants. A ministry enthusiastic to unite the community in religious and moral enterprise not only found little popular support but often met overt resistance. Presbyteries often had to adjourn their meetings for lack of three ministers to constitute a quorum. St. Joseph Presbytery held its very first meeting with only two ministers present and so was not legally constituted.[48] Even the Synod of Indiana, New School, was embarrassed because its attendance was so small that it feared it might be not only ineffective but disgraced in the public eye.[49] Perhaps the closest parallel to Presbyterian effort on the

47. Dickey, "An Address Delivered at the Home Missionary Anniversary in Cincinnati, November 1836," *HM, 10* (1837), 31.
48. John F. Kendall, *History of the Presbytery of Logansport* (Logansport, 1887) pp. 2–3.

Indiana frontier is the modern missionary effort of all the main-line denominations in the southern mountains. Here is the destitution, the paucity of male leadership in the churches, the sectarian intolerance, the apathy or downright aversion toward the reforming outlander.

There has been considerable discussion about the democracy of Presbyterian government. Buley called Presbyterianism "one of the most democratic polities of any of the churches on the frontier."[50] Sweet, on the other hand, counted Presbyterian polity as well as doctrine a handicap on the frontier[51] and said its appeal was aristocratic. Hall admitted that the equality of laymen and clergy in the presbytery was largely theoretical:

> Mr. Welden, Sen., and some other excellent old woodsmen, had seats as lay delegates. These, however, managed only the secular business of the Assembly; for instance, such as to bring in a pitcher of water, keep a small fire alive on the hearth, and contribute each twenty-five cents *cash* to the sub-treasury. Farther east, I am told, lay delegates are even more useful, volunteering to let down bars, open gates and the like, between the lodgings of the clergy and the chapel where the court is in session. Normally, it is *said*, the lay and clerical delegates are on equal footing in the House, both having a right to talk either sense or nonsense as long as they see fit; and yet, in practice, the lay members are not considered as on a par with the clerical ones. For instance, in debates, discussions and so forth, the commoners are never called— brother, except collectively under the appellation, brethren; and even then prime reference is intended to the clergy. But the commoners are termed variously, as "the worthy person or member"—"the good old man that has just spoken"—"Esquire

49. MIS, *1*, 281.
50. *Old Northwest*, 2, 446.
51. *Religion in American Culture*, pp. 115, 148.

Cleverly"—"Lawyer Counselton," etc., etc.: yet mostly they are all spoken to and about as plain— "Mister."[52]

There seems to have been no rotation of elders. Election to active duty on the session was counted for life or good behavior. Indianapolis church is the only church in Indianapolis Presbytery, Old School, to have elected and ordained deacons in 1839, and this may have been only upon the urging of the synod and presbytery.[53] Again and again the guiding hand of one or two leading elders is seen, as that of Isaac Coe in the calling of John R. Moreland to be pastor of First Church, Indianapolis; Samuel Merrill, in the calling of Henry Ward Beecher to Second Church, Indianapolis; and David H. Maxwell, in the calling of Baynard R. Hall to be principal of the new state seminary at Bloomington.[54] Presbytery affairs were generally in the hands of a few of the more faithful or more competent ministers. These leading elders and ministers were usually benevolent despots who felt that at least something had to be done to build up Zion without delay. The church government was democratic not because it closely represented the people or was responsive to them but because good order always allowed the conclusions or actions of the elite to be discussed and challenged. The challengers were few.

Presbytery meetings offered a real communion of the saints in early Indiana. There were stated meetings in spring and fall, plus as many special meetings as episcopal duty required. Stated meetings were held in rotation among the churches. If the distance was not too great, families and friends of the presbytery members might accompany. First there was the long ride through the forest:

52. *New Purchase*, pp. 234–35.
53. MIS, OS, *1*, 41, 59. MIP, *1*, 38.
54. James A. Woodburn, "Pioneer Presbyterians in Indiana," *Presbyterianism in Indiana* (Gary, 1926), p. 31. Isaac Coe, Indianapolis, 4 Nov. 1828, AHMS. Jane M. Ketcham, "History of Second Presbyterian Church during the Incumbency of Henry Ward Beecher" (MS in Indiana State Library), pp. 4–5.

Our party was increased at every ferry and cross path till it numbered twenty-two; enough to hold meeting on horseback. The time was mid Spring; and the old woods were glorying in the sylvan splendours of new dresses and decorations. The sun was, indeed, ardent, and rejoicing like one to run a race; but then the dense foliage spread a screen over the pathway, while the balmy breath of zephyrs, rich with perfume of wild flower and blossom, fanned our faces and sported with the forest leaf and spray. Beauteous birds and tribes of unseen animals and insects from every branch, and every bushy lair or cavern, were pouring forth choral symphonies of praise.

Was it wonderful, then, that Christians going to a spiritual congress, should be unable to restrain hymns of praise? Out upon rationalism, or any pseudo-ism that makes man *dumb* like—like—"beasts?" No; "insects?" No;—these in the woods God planted and nurtured for ages are vocal. "Like what then?" Like a German or a French Atheist.

Hymns then, as we rode, were sung; and, with heart and voice, in the solemn and joyous words of king David. God was felt to be there! His grand temple was around us! How like sons and daughters going home rejoicing! How like the Church in the wilderness. . . .

Arrived in due time at the place of the council, I was induced to remain a day and witness its proceedings. The weather being favourable, and no cabin large enough to accommodate the hundreds of spectators, many of whom had come more than a hundred miles, it was arranged to hold the sessions in the woods. Among the accommodations was a large wagon body placed on suitable timbers, to serve for a pulpit; and here, during the religious exercises, were seated all the clerical members—making with their aggregate weight a half a ton of theologians, if not of divinity. Here, also, during the secular business, was seated the President,—and supported by his scribes on the right and left.[55]

The first order of business at the presbytery was election of a moderator and clerk. Then the previous moderator read the standing rules and bylaws to the moderator elect and the presbytery heard the minutes of the last stated meeting. No matter how few the presbyters were, a full complement of committees was named: (1) to examine the session records from the churches; (2) to prepare certain reports for the General Assembly; (3) to collect and report special contributions from the churches and ministers. In a period of "free conversation on the state of religion" the presbytery inquired about all the churches under its care, and especially the host church. From this free conversation a committee gathered a "narrative on the state of religion" to forward to General Assembly. Most of these narratives are a historian's despair. They may reflect the mood either of the presbytery or of the writer, but they are heavy with generalities and stereotypes. The narrator usually concluded that the state of religion was low. He noted with gratitude attendance on the regular means of grace, progress of Sabbath schools and catechetical training, and some "periods of refreshing" in the churches. But he deplored poor attendance at the concert of prayer, lack of aggressive spirit in spreading the gospel, destitution of the churches, intemperance among the people, failure to support the benevolent boards or agencies, and neglect of family worship. These comments were liberally laced with Bible quotations. Isaac Reed and John Dickey did include a few facts in the narrative for the second meeting of Salem Presbytery, 9 April 1825:

> The Presbytery informs the Assembly, that through the blessings of the Head of the church, their infant churches are living in peace, and generally giving

55. Hall, pp. 452–54.

good attention to the preached gospel, as far as they are supplied with it. And though four fifths of them are destitute of a settled ministry, and three fourths are destitute of even stated supplies, still, to the praise of the Redeemer, they are nearly all yearly increasing in the number of their members. Eight new churches have been formed the last year. In three of our congregations the Spirit has been poured out— the saints have been revived—and sinners made to inquire after Christ and salvation. Two of them are in new settlements on our north western frontier; we have an immense territory, embracing near 180,000 population, and but 7 ordained ministers capable of public service, with only 3 licentiates. The assembly will see by our Presbyterial Report that our churches are 37, and we have the prospect of adding to their number the present year. We beg therefore for help.— A few Missionaries sent us from the Board of Missions, who would remain and settle in our bounds, could do us much good. We pray the assembly to consider us in this matter; our prospects have been long of a dark character, but are now fast brightening, and from the location of our churches, and the character and influence of many of their leading members, we think our state shall yet present a fair and lovely section of the Presbyterian church. Education is in general low, but we think it rising; we have one college seminary which is just beginning. It begins under encouraging auspices, and the state of morals, in our bounds, is, we believe, improving.[56]

The moderator made inquiry about education of youth for the ministry and the clerk dutifully recorded if candidates were many or few. This might lead to the exhortation to ministers to seek out likely candidates and to congregations to give financial

56. *Christian Traveller*, p. 198.

aid to "poor and pious" youths now in preparation. Of collections there was no end. Every member of the presbytery made a personal contribution to defray the presbytery's incidental expenses; in Salem Presbytery this was fifty cents per member per meeting. Representatives from the churches turned in money they had collected for the education fund, the fund to send commissioners to the Assembly, the missionary fund, the theological seminary. At every stated meeting there was a missionary sermon preached to the host congregation, visitors, and presbytery, followed by "a collection for the purpose of missions." Presbyters who arrived late were expected to give good reason for their tardiness. Special permission was required to leave before adjournment, this permission sometimes coupled with advice that no appointments ought to be made which conflicted with the presbytery meeting. Regular business was varied—ordaining a minister, electing a commissioner to the Assembly, suspending a member who would not "be reconciled to his brother on any reasonable terms."[57]

As the presbytery convened at one church after another within its bounds, it combined ecclesiastical business with social activity. Ministers and elders often brought their families to the meetings which lasted several days. Thus relatives and friends were happily reunited.[58] Presbyters and visitors joined in the services of prayer and praise. On the first day there was a meeting for prayer for all the churches and for that particular meeting. The retiring moderator customarily preached a sermon which was officially criticized as an item of the docket.[59] Presbytery members might be assigned to preach on temperance, slavery, education, support of the ministry, popery, or on a biblical or doctrinal theme. At each meeting the sacrament of the Lord's Supper was administered, and members were often added to the host church. Isaac Reed was examined and ordained by Transylvania Presbytery in October 1818.

57. Minutes of Muncie Presbytery, OS, *1*, 25.
58. Margaret DesChamps, "The Church as Social Center," *JPHS*, *31* (1953), 157–58.   59. MSP, *1*, 87, 89, 112–13.

That meeting continued from Wednesday through Sunday at the New Providence church and Reed recorded in his journal that it was a sacramental Sunday, with a large congregation and excellent preaching. The whole service was so solemn that many wept, and Reed was sure several young people were truly convicted. A married man and a young woman were baptized, and three brothers were received into the church.[60]

The synod met once a year but stayed in session for a week. Like the presbytery, it combined business, social interchange, and inspiration. October was the preferred time. The meeting usually began at candle-lighting—that is, with a service of worship in the evening. In many respects, the synod's meeting was like that of an enlarged presbytery. There was the election of moderator and clerk plus the reading of the rules and the minutes. Committees were named to examine the records of the presbyteries, prepare reports to the Assembly, consider judicial business, attend to various collections. There were at least two sermons: a missionary sermon with a collection taken up in favor of missions, and a *concio ad clerum* or sermon to the clergy on some subject previously assigned. Generally there were three or four sermons and a recommendation that each minister preach to his congregation on certain specified subjects before the next meeting of the synod.[61] The Lord's Supper was administered in a public gathering, and the expectations of revival were there. Mary Hovey wrote her sister in New York, "I attended the meeting of the Indiana Synod at Crawfordsville in October. Thirty men were present. On the Sabbath the Sacrament was administered to a house *full* of communicants. This was indeed an interesting season in the Valley of the Mississippi."[62] In 1828 Isaac Coe wrote to Absalom Peters about the surprising number of members added to the Vincennes church during the meeting of the synod. There were sixty-three received.[63] One synod meeting at New Albany set

60. *Christian Traveller*, p. 82.   61. MIS, *1*, 99, 123, 214.
62. Fountain County, in a letter to Mrs. Emily C. Foord, Cazenovia, New York, 8 March 1833.   63. Indianapolis, 4 Nov. 1828, AHMS.

off a revival which added 1,600 members to Protestant churches of the area, 400 to the Presbyterian.[64]

The synod differed from the presbytery by not examining candidates for the ministry and by having no direct oversight of the churches. Also, where the presbytery was content to appoint certain ministers for occasional preaching in vacant churches, the synod was concerned with missionary strategy for a vast area. The Indiana Missionary Society, whose officers were leaders in the synod, held its annual meeting just prior to the synod. An overture adopted at the very first meeting of the Indiana Synod in 1826 reads: "Whereas our Synod presents a great missionary field which ought to be occupied, and inasmuch as our people are more ready to contribute for missionary exertions within our bounds, therefore, Resolved that the General Assembly be requested to permit this Synod to manage its own missionary concerns; and that the Stated Clerk be directed to forward this resolution to the General Assembly."[65] The annual meetings or "anniversaries" for the temperance, tract, Bible, education, Sabbath school, and missionary societies were often held in connection with the synod. Agents for each would be duly heard and approved and a resolution passed urging support in the local congregations. Thus, on an October Saturday afternoon in 1830, the fifth meeting of the Synod of Indiana was in typical session at Madison:

> The special order of the day for this afternoon, viz: hearing the Agents of the American Tract Society, and of the American Sabbath School Union, was taken up, and Mr. Wilder was heard on behalf of the American Tract Society, and Rev. Samuel K. Sneed, on behalf of the American Sabbath School Union, and the Synod adopted the following resolutions, viz:

64. In a letter from Horace C. Hovey, Newburyport, Mass., to E. J. Hewitt, New Albany, 28 Sept. 1912, reprinted in Lucien V. Rule and Thomas B. Terhune, *History of Hutchinson Memorial Presbyterian Church of New Albany* (New Albany, 1937), pp. 23–27.   65. MIS, *1*, 12.

3.   CALEB MILLS, Founder of Wabash Academy

a

b

d

c

4. a. WILLIAM H. WISHARD,
   Early Elder at Greenwood

   b. JOHN FINLEY CROWE,
   Founder of Hanover Academy

   c. ISAAC COE,
   Founder of Sabbath Schools in
   Indianapolis

   d. BAYNARD HALL
   First Professor of Indiana
   University

a

b

c

d

5. a. JAMES A. CARNAHAN,
   Missionary to the Upper Wabash

   b. DAVID MONFORT,
   Stalwart of the "Old School"

   c. THOMAS CLELAND,
   First Presbyterian Preacher of
   Record

   d. EDMUND O. HOVEY,
   Professor at Wabash College

   e. MARTIN M. POST,
   Pioneer Preacher in Northern
   Indiana

e

6.   ISAAC REED, The Christian Traveler

1. Resolved, That a judicious, systematic distribution of Tracts to our entire population, is greatly calculated to promote the interest of religion within the bounds of this Synod.

2. That it is very earnestly requested that the members of the Synod cooperate with the A.T.S. in carrying forward this work in their own congregations.

3. Resolved, That the Synod have heard with devout gratitude to God, of the truly Christian enterprise of the American Sunday School Union, to establish a Sabbath School in every destitute place, throughout the Valley of the Mississippi, within two years; and they do most earnestly recommend to the Pastors and Sessions of all our churches and congregations, to present this subject to their people, and solicit their prayers, labours, and contributions, to aid the Society in the accomplishment of this important object.

4. Resolved, That the ministers and members of our churches be recommended to devote the afternoons of the Sabbath, ordinarily to Sabbath Schools.

5. Resolved, That the members of our churches and congregations, except those advanced to extreme old age, be earnestly and affectionately recommended to unite themselves into Bible Class, for their mutual improvement in the Knowledge of God's word, with a special view to qualifying them for Sabbath School Teachers; and that it be enjoined upon the ministers and sessions of our churches to take proper measures on this subject.

6. Resolved, That competent laymen be encouraged (where circumstances will admit,) to go into destitute neighborhoods and constitute and conduct Sabbath Schools. . . .

The Synod adjourned to meet on Monday morning at 9 o'clock. Concluded with prayer.[66]

66. Ibid., pp. 86, 87, 103.

The Societies multiplied to the point of embarrassment. The synod's time was consumed with detailed reports ranging from the instruction of the Miami Indians to Bible distribution among sailors and boatmen. Agents for each cause traveled among the churches. The only solution seemed to be some systematic plan of promotion. This was done rather carefully by assigning each major benevolent cause two or three months for promotion and collection in the churches, a benefit to both the agents and the congregations.[67] Of all the worthy causes of the Indiana Synod, colleges and seminaries were the most strenuously promoted and the least well supported. Whether at Hanover or at New Albany, the seminary was especially deep in debt. The synod named an agent, then named an agent in each presbytery, then named all ministers as agents, then assigned dollar quotas to the presbyteries. None of these devices was sufficient to bring even minimal support to the school.

In regular business session the synod might deliver itself on any subject. Slavery was a favorite and dozens of pages of the records are filled with long resolutions against slavery and finally against slaveholders. All the concerns of the benevolent societies were treated in turn. As the population grew, the synod was occupied in setting up new presbyteries. Ministers needed urging to do their duties, and people needed urging to support the preachers in their labors. Any phase of the common life of the church might be grounds for exhortation. At the fourth meeting, in 1829, the Indiana Synod considered that perennial concern of the kingdom, the Doctor of Divinity degree. They resolved not to enter any man's degree beside his name on the synod records, because they deemed honorary titles among churchmen inappropriate and directly contrary to the simplicity of God's precepts.[68]

When ministers were scarce, churches few, and roads poor, being a good presbyter was likely to be demanding. The first

67. Ibid., pp. 282–84. MIS, OS, *1*, 43. MSP, NS, *1*, 92.
68. MIS, *1*, 57. MMP, *1*, 130.

presbytery formed in Indiana was Salem, which met first in April 1824. Within eighteen months it had met in Charlestown (twce), Indianapolis, Washington, Bloomington, Bethle-hem, Vincennes, Pisgah, and Madison. Most of the members were needed to conduct business, and travel was by horseback. Consider the lot of Isaac Reed, who rode horseback fifty miles to the presbytery at Washington on 5 April 1825. He preached the opening sermon and convened the presbytery for the election of John M. Dickey as moderator. Four ministers and eight elders were present. Reed and Dickey were appointed to prepare a presbyterial report, to prepare a narrative of the state of religion, and to form missionary districts within the bounds of the presbytery. Then the bylaws, which Reed had helped prepare, were read and the evening was spent in special prayer for the outpouring of the Spirit. Next day it was agreed that, as soon as business had ended at Washington, the presbytery should adjourn to meet at Bloomington (at least fifty miles horseback) to ordain and install Baynard Hall, Mr. Reed to preach the sermon. There followed considerable business in which Reed had his full share, including the presentation of his semi-annual fifty cents to the presbytery fund—this during the period of which he reported that he had not received one dollar in money from his congregation for two years. An additional meeting was set for Bethlehem church for the last Friday in June to ordain and install Mr. Tilly H. Brown—Mr. Reed to preach the sermon. In the answers to petitions for supply, Mr. Reed was assigned to supply one Sabbath in Green County, one in Putnam, one in Shiloh church, and one at Paris, all before the next stated meeting of the presbytery. Then the presbytery moved directly to Bloomington to what was almost certainly a three-day ordination meeting complete with sacrament. While at Bloomington, the presbytery received an incidental request for supply at Crawfordsville. Mr. Reed was directed to supply one Sabbath at that place. Also at Bloomington, Reed, Crowe, and Hall were appointed a committee to revise and publish an abridgment of Jerham's *Conversations on Baptism*, previously abridged by Reed. There were six ordinations in Indiana in 1825; Reed preached at four.[69] He may have been "a queer specimen of theology" as Julia Merrill Moores[70] called him, but he certainly was active. Similarly, at the first meeting of the Indiana Synod, John Finley Crowe was named to four synod committees the first day. Next day he was named treasurer of the synod, named to committees three times more, and named as alternate to preach before the synod. On the third day he was named to a position of interpreter of his labors, membership on the historical committee.[71]

At every level, Presbyterian church government was concerned with disciplinary action. This is a commonplace of frontier church history. Literally thousands of cases are recorded. A classic statement of their significance is William Warren Sweet's address, "The Churches as Moral Courts of the Frontier."[72] The session of the local Presbyterian church was in fact a court. If charges were properly made concerning a member, that member was duly tried. If no complaint was filed but the misdemeanor was generally known, the session might take up the case upon "common fame." The accused had full right to know all charges and specifications, to obtain counsel, to call witnesses, and in general to present his defense. Further, if there appeared grounds for appeal, he might appeal the decision to the presbytery, the synod, and even to the General Assembly.

One of the simplest cases on record is reported by James Crawford of Delphi: "A young lady of our church was induced by extra efforts to attend and participate in a dance and before the fact was known to the session she presented a humble confession in writing to the church which with her consent I read publicly then read the Gen. Assemblies condemnation of that

69. MSP, *1*, 18–24. *Christian Traveller*, pp. 146, 205–06.
70. "Early Times," *IMH, 8*, 136.
71. MIS, *1*, 2–7.
72. *CH, 2* (1933), 3–21.

amusement from the A's digest and made known the full concurrence of this session in the sentiments expressed by the Assembly."[73] Whiskey was among the most common trouble-makers. A typical example of the difficulty it caused was recorded in 1853. A certain Andrew Glenn had been admonished for intemperance and had confessed his sin. But despite the encouragement to repentance offered by his fellow church members, Mr. Glenn refused to mend his ways. The session ruled, therefore, that he be excluded from communion of the church.[74] Sometimes domestic troubles found their way into the church court. Katherine Hadden of Sugar Creek church in Shelby County was charged with "applying for and obtaining a divorce from your lawful husband contrary to the word of God." Mrs. Hadden confessed the offense but pleaded the abuse of her husband as justification. The session read Matthew 5:32 to her and suspended her pending advice from the presbytery. The Presbytery of Indianapolis commented:

> No crime, except the crime of adultery, relieves a woman from the relation of a wife to her husband. But when her personal safety, or the maintainance of herself and children demand it, she may take advantage of a divorce, so far as these objects are secured; but she is still to consider herself by the law of God, as truly a wife to her husband as ever, (although she is not permitted to live with him as such.) and is no more at liberty to think of marrying another, than she would had they lived in happiness together.[75]

In another case of separation, the wife testified that her husband took things not belonging to him, for example a chain and some corn. Further, he stole a pumpkin and made her

73. 10 July 1832, AHMS.
74. From session records, Mount Pleasant church, Marion County, 11 Dec. 1853.
75. From session records, Sugar Creek church, Shelby County, Sept. 1846, pp. 14–18.

cook it for him and ate it. The session was impressed with these reasons and sought advice of the presbytery, but the presbytery decided they were insufficient. She was suspended from the church.[76]

Presbyteries gave much counsel to the churches about disciplinary procedures. The Salem Presbytery affirmed that an offended member was to act as directed by Matthew 18:15–17.[77] This was too hard for Mrs. Henderson of Salem church, who "felt herself aggrieved with one of the sisters of the church." She said that unless the offending sister "made to her a satisfactory written acknowledgement" she would not worship or commune with her. The session worked with Mrs. Henderson patiently but finally acted: "It is hereby resolved that she be suspended from the privileges of the Church until she manifests satisfactory signs of repentance."[78] Most of the presbyteries took a strong stand on Sabbath-keeping. The fourth commandment was considered "of binding and perpetual obligation." This prohibited Sunday team-driving and social visiting, and even Saturday-night visiting. Only errands of mercy were acceptable as reasons for Sunday travel.[79] Preachers were to take care not to ride unnecessarily on the Sabbath and the sessions were to keep an eye on everybody else. The day of "fasting, humiliation, and prayer on account of the sin of the profanation of the Sabbath" ought to be observed by assembling the people and reading to them the resolution of the Assembly on this subject.[80]

Both churches and presbyteries came to make total abstinence a condition of church membership. Most of the new churches formed by American Home Missionary Society mis-

76. Joseph Ranney, *History of the Presbyterian Church in Delphi* (Lafayette, 1875), p. 10.
77. MSP, *1*, 70.
78. "Records of Salem Presbyterian Church," as copied by Genealogical Records Committee, Daughters of the American Revolution, Salem, p. 10.
79. MIP, NS, *1*, 20–22.
80. MSP, *1*, 77, 86. MMP, *1*, 127–30. MLP, *1*, 83.

sionaries were formed on this basis. For example, the Presbyterian church at LaPorte made the pledge a condition of church membership when it was founded in 1832. In 1827 the Salem Presbytery resolved that the members of that presbytery would be total abstainers and urged their congregations to do the same. In 1829 Salem urged the sessions to watch the conduct of members in this respect, especially the admission of new members. The resolution urging voluntary abstinence was to be read to all the congregations in 1830. Inquiry in 1831 disclosed only two or three church members within Salem Presbytery who made or sold whiskey. Then in 1832 the presbytery urged the sessions to induce abstinence by "all those motives which the Gospel holds out" and then excommunicate those who would not hear. This action was to be read in the churches.[81]

Cases of discipline came to the presbytery because a member of the presbytery was involved, or by appeal from the sessions. A good example of a case appealed is that of Brother Sidney Muzzy of Knightstown. Mr. Muzzy evidently disapproved of the assignment of pews in church. When one family put a door on the family pew, Brother Muzzy secretly took the door down, refused to return it, to let anybody else return it, or to refer the matter to the trustees. The session charged him somewhat hotly, and Muzzy appealed to the Presbytery of Indianapolis, Old School. The presbytery sustained the charges, though it reported the language as somewhat harsh, and resolved "that Brother Muzzy be affectionately admonished to act more discreetly and considerately for the future, studying the things that make for peace and the welfare of souls." But Muzzy was not to be put off. He appealed to the Indiana Synod, where the case was heard in September 1849. The synod's decision is a model of mediation. The appeal was sustained in part because the language of the charge seemed to accuse Mr. Muzzy of felony which was not warranted. The charges were sustained in part because Muzzy had acted rashly, and the synod admonished him and all concerned to be more considerate and peaceable.

81. MSP, *1*, 51, 70, 78, 123, 150. MMP, *1*, 64–65, 108–09. MIP, NS, *1*, 22.

Further, the synod expressed regret that the pew door was placed there without authority and the concurrence of the congregation.[82]

Cases involving ministers were likely to be much more tedious. And the presbyteries seemed to have a kind of personality of their own regarding litigation. Madison and Logansport Presbyteries were comparatively harmonious. On the other hand, John Kendall said of Lake Presbytery:

> None of our six Presbyteries, nor any Presbytery with which your Historian has had acquaintance, has equaled Lake, in trials, appeals, complaints, dissents, investigations. Seventy successive pages are taken up, in the record of one trial. The dreary monotony of such a record, and especially the fact of being condemned to be an actor in it, is fearful to contemplate. Whether this Presbytery was more devoted to law and order or whether it embraced an unusually refractory set of preachers, elders, church members and churches, will probably never be known. Certain it is, I think, that they never shrank from any duty because it was disagreeable.[83]

In the more cantankerous days of Indianapolis Presbytery, during the early 1830s, N. H. Bishop observed that the presbytery never had been in harmony and that at this time it was especially incapable of doing business. He believed the members were imprudent men and that they had no confidence in one another. Things had reached the point where, had he been able to do so, he would have simply dissolved the Presbytery of Indianapolis.[84]

The whole structure of Presbyterian government in America was crippled by the Old School–New School division, and in Indiana it was pathetic to see a synod dismembered shortly

82. MIP, OS, *1*, 367–68, 374.
83. Kendall, *History Presbytery of Logansport*, p. 9.
84. Oxford, Ohio, 22 Feb. 1833, AHMS.

after its founding. The reason for the division was the difference of opinion among American Presbyterians from the beginning. Leonard J. Trinterud has demonstrated the cleavage between the English and the Scotch-Irish Presbyterians.[85] That conflict was sharpened as some Presbyterians became suspicious of the doctrinal formulations of certain New England theologians. Samuel Hopkins and Nathaniel Taylor were among those charged with errors, though not precisely the same ones. The critical doctrines concerned sin, human ability, and salvation.[86] The conservatives counted the New England theology especially dangerous at a time when the church was being filled with young ministers who thought this theology was the latest and the best.[87]

Princeton became the center for the Scotch-Irish group, which was strong for the federal theology and for strict subscription to the Westminster Confession. Many of the Scotch-Irish pastors who trained young ministers in their frontier homes and "log colleges" took this position, as did the Indiana Theological Seminary at Hanover. On the other hand, the English Presbyterians were often trained at Yale, Andover, Union, Auburn, or Lane. Generally, the New England men were hotly opposed to slavery and favorable to missions under the voluntary or nondenominational societies. The Old School men hedged on the issue of slavery[88] in the interest of peace with the southern wing of the church and favored missions directly under the control of the General Assembly. No lines were exact. In general, it was the conservative, Scotch and Scotch-Irish, anti-abolition, rigidly Presbyterian Old School against the experimental, English and New English,

85. *Forming American Tradition*, pp. 261–64, and passim.
86. For a brief treatment of Taylor and the New England theology see Roland H. Bainton, *Yale and the Ministry* (New York, Harper, 1957), pp. 96–112.
87. William A. Brown, "Changes in the Theology of American Presbyterianism," *American Journal of Theology, 10* (1906), 387–411.
88. W. E. Dodd, "Profitable Fields of Investigation in American History," *AHR, 18* (1913), 522–36.

antislavery, loosely Presbyterian New School. Slavery was not a major factor in the division of the Presbyterian Church in the Old Northwest; Indiana members were practically unanimous in their opposition to it. In the division of the national General Assembly, however, slavery was an important factor.[89]

From the time of the formation of the American Home Missionary Society in 1826 and its notable success, the struggle between the two groups heightened. The conservatives seem to have been jealous and fearful of the success of New England in recruiting and training ministerial candidates, some of them native sons from the West. Then they saw these young men whom they feared to be of questionable orthodoxy being sent out through the missionary societies with Presbyterian money.[90] They were forming Presbyterian churches and infiltrating the church courts, a source of genuine concern to the Scotch-Irish. Control of the missionary operation became a symbol of power. By 1830 contention within the Presbyterian Church was so hot that efficiency in evangelism or church program was much impaired. Western churchmen saw the catastrophe in the making. They urged that the General Assembly and the missionary societies unite at the top on some reasonable ground. Then they urged that if there must be a split in the East, let there be one Western Missionary Society related to both and so preserve the unity of the West. Finally they suggested that frontier presbyteries should remain united and receive mission aid from either or both mission bodies.[91] None of these solutions for the West was effected. From 1831 to 1836 the New School party held the majority vote at the General

89. Irving S. Kull, "Presbyterian Attitudes toward Slavery," *CH,* 7 (1938), 101–14. C. Bruce Staiger, "Abolitionism and the Presbyterian Schism of 1837–1838," *MVHR, 36* (1949), 391–414. James H. Johnston, *Ministry of Forty Years, p.* 19. MIS, *1,* 257–58. Elwyn A. Smith, "The Role of the South in the Presbyterian Schism of 1837–1838," *CH, 29* (1960), 44–63.

90. Goodykoontz, *Home Missions,* pp. 172–80. Gillett, *History Presbyterian Church, 2,* 228.

91. Drury, p. 84. James H. Johnston, John M. Dickey, and the Madison Presbytery were for these alternatives to division. See Samuel G. Lowry, Greensburgh, 20 Dec. 1830, AHMS.

Assembly every year but one. They were self-confident and assured. The Old School party feared for the cause of orthodoxy and the future course of the church. In 1837 there was an Old School majority. That majority acted on the basis of their darkest fears. In a drastic action they cut off four whole synods of the church (509 ministers, 599 churches and some 60,000 members) without warning and without formal trial. The synods exscinded were heavily New School; their exclusion would guarantee direction of the remaining body by the Old School. Now the whole church had to divide in terms of allegiance either to the Old School Assembly or to the New School Assembly that was promptly formed. To a modern student their differences seem small and certainly negotiable, but to many of the participants the issues were crucial and the struggle bitter.

In Indiana, however, the lines were less clear. Faced with the needs of the raw new state, ministers felt that the issues of the East were less pressing. When a missionary was supported in Indiana by the American Home Missionary Society it did not necessarily mean that he was a champion of the "New Divinity" or even that he was a New School man. John Finley Crowe of Hanover was Old School but was aided by an American Home Missionary Society commission. Even W. W. Martin, solidly Old School, reported the revival at his Livonia church through the pages of the New School *Indiana Religious Intelligencer*.[92] Further, he served with Isaac Reed and John Dickey as an officer of the Indiana Missionary Society to locate missionaries of the American Home Missionary Society when they arrived in Indiana.[93] The Synod of Indiana did not seek division. There is sorrow written over its proceedings of these years. New School records speak of the Old School as "friends of reform" and of the Assemblies of 1837 and 1838 which excluded them as "Reformed Assemblies."[94] The Synod of

92. Vol. 1, pp. 137–44.
93. Edson, p. 258. James H. Johnston, Madison, 14 Aug. 1826, AHMS.
94. MIS, *1*, 256, 260.

Indiana, Old School, carefully states that while it adheres to the Old School Assembly it does not count approval of the acts of the Assemblies of 1837 and 1838 as tests of membership. "We do not recognize as a test of membership in the Presbyterian church any other than the confession of faith and constitution long since adopted as such by the whole church."[95] By special vote of the Old School synod, Ransom Hawley was "excused from voting on the resolutions declaring adherence to the General Assembly; and also on the resolutions declaring certain ministers no longer members of the Presbyterian Church in the United States of America."[96].

In the Indianapolis Presbytery the division took shape along classic lines, and this presbytery affords the best case study. The first book of the Minutes of Indianapolis Presbytery (1831–37) was lost for years, and even a student of history is inclined to wish it had remained lost. It preserves a most unlovely record of strife and wasted effort. There were six ministers in Indianapolis Presbytery when it was formed in 1831; three were Old School in their sympathy and three were New School. David Monfort was pastor at Franklin and Hopewell, being of Dutch Reformed background and a graduate of Princeton Seminary in 1817. John R. Moreland was pastor of First Presbyterian Church of Indianapolis, Scotch-Irish and Kentucky trained in Transylvania University and the manse of Thomas Cleland. He was described on one occasion as just the man to speak to Hoosiers in the language they understood, on another as a Kentucky "ranter."[97] William Sickels studied theology at Princeton and came to Indiana as a missionary of the General Assembly's Board of Missions. These were three champions of the Old School and eventually they carried the presbytery. The New School men were all missionaries of the American

95. MIS, OS, *1*, 17–18. This is in fact an overstatement. Affirmation of the Confession of Faith or the constitution is not asked as a condition of Presbyterian Church membership.
96. MIS, OS, *1*, 33.
97. Isaac Coe, 4 Nov. 1828, AHMS. Samuel Merrill, in a letter to his brother David (no place indicated), 4 Dec. 1828.

Home Missionary Society: Jeremiah Hill in Owen County, Samuel G. Lowry in Decatur County, and William W. Woods at Greenwood. All three had been trained in Tennessee and all three were effective frontier pastors.[98]

The fight was on from the opening meeting of the presbytery. Typically, the American Home Missionary Society was sending out more ministers than was the Assembly's Board. The Old School ministers felt that they must rule this influx of New School men for the safety of their presbytery and of the whole Presbyterian Church. At the very first session Eliphalet Kent presented himself for membership. He was a Yankee born in Vermont and educated in Massachusetts and at Auburn Seminary in New York. Since his papers from the Rutland Association were in order and he had already been serving as a missionary in Shelby and Bartholomew Counties for almost two years, he was accepted. But the Old School men of the presbytery had further grounds for concern. James R. Wheelock, a New England man full of the New Divinity, was seated as a corresponding member at that very first meeting of the presbytery. He had settled down as missionary at Greensburg and given a clue to his background by sending word back East, "We have let part of our silver spoons go for a cow."[99] He was a member in good standing of the Windsor Association and it appeared only a matter of time until he would apply for admission. John Todd, once suspended by the Kentucky Synod for heresy, was soon to settle in Marion County, another missionary of the American Home Missionary Society.

The Old School forces of the Indianapolis Presbytery were not to be overcome. If the New School men were more numerous, the Old School men were more faithful presbyters and better strategists. Vacant churches sent elder delegates to

98. John M. Dickey, *Early History of the Presbyterian Church in Indiana Giving Biographies of Ministers and Annals of the Churches* (Indianapolis, 1848), *1*, 1, 57, 79; *2*, 3. *Centennial First Church, Indianapolis*, pp. 82–83. Elizabeth M. Wishard, *William Henry Wishard, A Doctor of the Old School* (Indianapolis, Hollenbeck, 1920), pp. 290–91.

99. 31 Jan. 1831, AHMS.

the presbytery, and these elders enjoyed opposing novelty, especially by Yankees. One of the earliest resolutions passed by a safe Old School majority stated "that every minister or licentiate from another Presbytery or corresponding body, applying to be received as a member of this Presbytery, shall submit to an examination on the doctrines of our Confession of Faith, provided any two members of Presbytery shall require it."[100] While that Old School majority was at hand in 1831, William Sickels and two elders were named a committee to formulate the position of the presbytery on missions. The bias of the resolution adopted was plainly for the General Assembly's Board of Missions and against the American Home Missionary Society or any cooperation or merger with that body. No voluntary association of irresponsible individuals, as the Old School presbytery described the mission societies, should be permitted to conduct missionary operations within the Presbyterian Church. Only the Assembly's Board of Missions could maintain purity of doctrine and discipline.[101]

James Wheelock was to be the test case. On 5 April 1832 Wheelock presented his dismission and recommendations from Windsor Association and asked to be received as a member of Indianapolis Presbytery. He was an unrepentant Yankee and an effective one. He was preaching regularly at Greensburg and eight other places in the county. It was his opinion "that certain views of many Presbyterian preachers and their preaching have done more to prejudice the minds of the people at large against Presbyterianism—to make Methodists, New Lights, Cumberland Presbyterians, Free-Will Baptists, United Brethren, etc., than all other causes put together." He stressed the freedom and accountability of the sinner, that all may come if they will, "that the Holy Spirit is not granted to give men any new powers or capacities as moral agents but to convince them of sin and to make them willing to do what they before had power to do but would not."[102] Two members of

100. MIP, *1*, 20.   102. Wheelock, Greensburg, 27 Aug. 1832, AHMS.
101. Ibid., pp. 20–23.

the presbytery promptly asked that he be examined on theology. But at that meeting the majority was New School. It was moved and carried that the entire standing rule requiring such a special examination of an ordained man be rescinded. Wheelock answered the constitutional questions and was received. An attempt by John R. Moreland to enroll the presbytery as an education society auxiliary to the Board of Education of the Assembly was defeated. Wheelock prepared the report on missions, which was markedly favorable toward the American Home Missionary Society and a sharp revision of the stand of the presbytery six months before. Presbytery now said that the American Home Missionary Society was supplying the churches on the frontier with an able ministry and laboring in the best interest of the Presbyterian Church.[103]

The balance of power was a shifting thing, however, and in October 1832 the rule was reinstated requiring that applicants for transfer should be examined on theology in case two members requested it. This was quickly followed by another action requiring a two-thirds majority to rescind a standing rule of the presbytery. Nor was Wheelock's battle won. In November of 1832 he was charged before Presbytery by an elder as follows:

> Spec. 1 That he, Mr. Wheelock has stated, that the sufferings of the wicked after death, consists in their being deprived of the enjoyment of sensible objects and social intercourse, and not in the infliction of divine vengeance.
>
> Spec. 2 He denies the doctrine of federal representation, and says that Adam was not the federal head of his posterity.
>
> Spec. 3 He denies that Adam's sin in eating the forbidden fruit was imputed to his posterity.
>
> Spec. 4 He denies that Christ paid the debt of suffering for sinners, or obeyed the law in their room

103. MIP, *1*, 46–47.

and stead, so that the merits of that obedience can be imputed to sinners for their righteousness.

Spec. 5 He says that if believers are justified by a righteousness commensurate with the claims of the law, salvation is not of grace but of debt.

Spec. 6 He has falsely stated, that the cause of opposition against him, in the Greensburg Presbyterian Church, was that he would not preach that hell was lined with the souls of infants.[104]

To all the specifications Wheelock pleaded "not true." The trial proceeded for three days in November and was adjourned to be taken up in January of 1833. All the evidence and testimony, along with Wheelock's newest statement of his doctrinal views, was submitted to the presbytery for judgment. Evidently all the Old School elders were present. All the specifications against Wheelock were sustained. Wheelock announced his intention to appeal to the synod. There was a contest over his right to appeal. The Old School majority wanted to press on to a decision, in effect a sentence, for Wheelock. However, the moderator was a New School man who would neither put the question nor allow an appeal from his decision. Finally the four New School ministers and one elder did an amazing thing. They walked out of the presbytery leaving it without a moderator or a quorum! For two regular meetings the New School men boycotted the presbytery and it could not conduct any business for lack of a quorum.

Meanwhile the synod had taken up the Wheelock case in a procedure which must have occupied three days. Its final action noted that New School language and doctrinal expressions were widespread in the Presbyterian Church and ought to be tolerated to a degree. Since Wheelock had been incautious and had given undue offense, he was "solemnly and affectionately admonished" to make use of "good and acceptable words" in his public ministry. However, Wheelock's

104. Ibid., pp. 75–76.

prosecutors were also admonished to refrain from reckless charges against a minister.[105] Fourteen members of the synod signed the record in formal dissent against letting Wheelock off so easily, Monfort and Sickels among them. Moreland had died in 1832.

The synod had directed the Presbytery of Indianapolis to meet; therefore, the New School members returned, somewhat chastened. William W. Woods was admonished for walking out of his office as moderator. Two additional ministers were received, one Old School in sympathy and the other New School. But four days later Michael Remley of Salem Presbytery applied for admission and, being an American Home Missionary Society man, was faced by two members requiring he be examined on theology. He simply withdrew his application. Before the year was out, the Old School party in the presbytery had consolidated its control. A series of resolutions indicated their intention that the New School party should not rise again. Established churches were not allowed to apply to the American Home Missionary Society for pastors; new churches founded by Society missionaries would not be admitted to the presbytery.[106]

New School men left the presbytery. In 1835 Eliphalet Kent reported: "Such are the strenuous measures pursued by our presbytery at present that I am fearful that I shall be obliged to leave the Churches to which I now minister before long. All the ministers but myself in this Presbytery who ranked among the New School have left the bounds. The consequence is that there are two or three churches near here that are dwindling to nothing. They are discouraged. A fearful responsibility rests somewhere."[107] When the time came in 1837, Indianapolis Presbytery methodically condemned "certain errors in doctrine held and practiced by many in the Presbyterian Church." With unseemly calm they wrote off the Plan of Union and the four synods of Genessee, Geneva, Utica, and Western Reserve

105. MIS, *1*, 154–56.   107. Greenwood, 27 Nov. 1835, AHMS.
106. MIP, *1*, 104–06.

as having almost subverted their wholesome system of discipline and doctrine and brought them under an influence that was irresponsible and foreign.[108]

Indianapolis Presbytery aptly illustrates the problems of the Old School–New School split. Wheelock was a brilliant and irresponsible Yankee reformer, confident in the power of New England schoolbooks to cure Kentuckyisms and in the power of his theology to sweep the West before him. In his own opinion, he was not denying the Westminster Confession but was making sense out of it. He was slow to connect himself with a presbytery and slower still to be subject to his brethren. When a majority made up of two ministers and five elders sustained the charges of heresy against him, his answer was to call a public meeting of citizens at the courthouse of his home town, where they expressed their confidence in him and affirmed that public opinion should be consulted in selection of a minister.[109] Wheelock could organize and lead a camp meeting with an attendance of 800, as he did in Greensburg. At the same time, half his congregation wanted to rise up and throw him out. One big factor in the division was the independence of missionaries from the eastern societies. There were not many Wheelocks, but there were enough young men with disturbing thoughts and independent attitudes to worry the Old School men.

The history of Indianapolis Presbytery also illustrates well the response of the Old School. They included some of the finest churchmen and some of the most devoted Christians. They saw heresy in this new theology, and the heresy appeared deadly. What was worse, the heretics were moving into position to control the Presbyterian Church. The motivation of the Old School was a mixture of fear and duty. In retrospect their fears seem unwarranted.

The tragedy had to be played to its conclusion, however. The Old School told its story through the *Western Presbyterian Herald;* the New School organ was the *Watchman of the Valley.*

108. MIP, *1*, 309–11.
109. Wheelock, Greensburg, 10 Jan. 1833, AHMS.

Hanover College and the Indiana Theological Seminary were Old School; the New School supported Wabash College and Lane Seminary. The southern settlers inclined to be Old School, but so much of the founding of churches had been done by eastern societies that the two bodies were nearly equal in size. A few cities like Madison, Indianapolis, and New Albany were large enough to provide for Old School and New School congregations without serious damage to congregational life. Not so in most places. The most painful part of the disintegration of the denomination was the tearing apart of particular congregations. Churches with a handful of members divided doggedly and endured the tension over who got the church property, who got the church records, and who got the church name. New School members visiting their former brethren for worship were not invited to communion in the First Presbyterian Church of Indianapolis.[110] Samuel G. Lowry, traveling as an agent of the American Home Missionary Society, stopped to spend Sunday in a church he had established and had supplied for years. Three Old School ministers were conducting a sacramental meeting. They did not accord Lowry the least courtesy as a minister or invite him to take part in the service.[111]

The Old School forces took the initiative. Very often their procedure was to incite suspicion in the mind of an elder or a small group already disaffected in the local congregation. The tragic history of their campaign was reported by church after church.

> There is one man in the congregation who pretends to be an "Old School" man and says he wishes an old school minister. He was also one of the founders of the church and feels that he has a kind of right to govern as he pleases.[112]
>
> I believe there was entire harmony as it regards these matters among this people until a paper, called

110. Moores, "Early Times," *IMH, 8,* 139.
111. Lowry, Crawfordsville, 4 July 1838, AHMS.
112. P. S. Cleland, Jeffersonville, 3 Oct. 1837, AHMS.

"The Standard" found its way to the houses of a few. This paper, which is published at Hanover, in this State, is well calculated to continue, and widen the difficulties in the Presbyterian Church.[113]

In a neighborhood 4 miles from the place of meeting live 5 families one of them related to one of the Elders of the 1st Church in Madison. Not one of them are professors yet this Elder 2 weeks ago wrote to his son-in-law to "be cautious of Wilder" "He is a bad man, a new school man, we would not let him preach in our church." These families were in favor with Presbyterianism but after this letter they did not go to Meeting. Queer—would that Elder rather have his children perish, than be brought to repentance by new school efforts?[114]

An agent from the Assembly's Board has visited the church and I fear has not done too much good. Two or three of the members have been made to feel and believe that wisdom must die with that venerable board and that the A.H.M.S. will compell the Presbyterian churches and Presbyteries vi et armis, to receive into their bosoms her heterodox missionaries unless the board shall by the grace of God, be enabled to stop her progress.[115]

I fear the New and Old School question is doing its work here especially in the Thorntown Church. . . . The kings of Persia were delighted when the States of Greece were warring with each other because they knew they were wasting and devouring each other without expense or trouble to themselves. But can it be that those kings were better pleased than is the Pope of Rome to hear of the deadly warfare that is carried on in the Presbyterian Church in these United

113. Claiborne Young, Boone County, 31 Dec. 1834, AHMS.
114. Moses Wilder, Jefferson County, 7 April 1834, AHMS.
115. Leander Cobb, Charlestown, 27 April 1831, AHMS.

States. I say *deadly* warfare because in various ways
much very much spiritual life is destroyed.[116]

We have but one man only, who knows the world
is nearly all wrong but himself and a few others, we
have great reason to Bless God that so much harmony
prevail among us.[117]

The difficulty between old and new School has
broke out in all its worst aspects. One of the principal
Elders in Shelbyville Church takes a warm part
against me. It is with much difficulty that business
can be done in Session. The church as a body, so far
as I know, are satisfied with me. I cannot feel that I
am Commissioned to waste my strength in contending
with the Church.[118]

Division has marred the beauty of Zion. New
Providence Church, embracing formerly 40 members
is reduced to about 20 and instead of being as formerly an energetic and prosperous Church, she has
become measurably enfeebled and inactive by discouragement.[119]

The crisis at Bedford is a classic example of Old School tactics.
Solomon Kittredge, the pastor, was a New Hampshire boy and
a graduate of Andover Seminary. He came to Indiana as a
missionary of the American Home Missionary Society in 1832.
After a brief period of understudy with Benjamin Cressy at
Salem, Kittredge went to Bedford, and there he stayed. His was
a vital church filled to overflowing with young people. A new
meetinghouse was under construction, temporarily delayed for
lack of funds. In 1839 came the invasion:

An Old School brother . . . was determined on
rending my church in twain. . . A young minister
was sent here to declare the Bedford Church vacant

116. Claiborne Young, Boone County, 15 April 1835, AHMS.
117. Jeremiah Hill, Owen County, 1 April 1833, AHMS.
118. Eliphalet Kent, Shelbyville, 1 May 1833, AHMS.
119. Idem, Greenwood, 6 April 1839, AHMS.

and to supply them a part of his time. Books and pamphlets and papers of a party character were put in circulation among my people. After these and other preparatory steps of a like character had been taken, a sacramental meeting . . . was appointed in the Bedford Church without consulting either the Session, the members of the Church, or myself. . . . Father Martin (as he is called here, being one of the oldest ministers in this section of the country) . . . made a public statement respecting the New School heresy and the necessary measures that had been taken to cleanse the Church, and at the close took the names of all those who wished to "remain Presbyterian." . . . I made no direct opposition to the efforts the Old School brethren were making, said as little as possible on the subject of New and Old School but endeavoured to keep the minds of my people on things of higher importance. Seldom have I suffered greater distress in mind than during this season of trial. . . Only six of the members of my Church gave their names to the Old School.[120]

Time began to heal the breach. While the Old School synod of Northern Indiana was meeting at Logansport in October 1845, the New School synod was also meeting there. It was the Old School synod which sent a committee suggesting a joint synodical prayer meeting. The union meeting was held.[121] In 1849 the Presbytery of Salem, Old School, could say very frankly that the Old School Presbyterian church of Salem was about dead and it would be better if the local members would join the New School Presbyterians.[122]

Thirty years after Indianapolis Presbytery had divided with somber talk of heresy and subversion, the Indianapolis Presbytery, Old School, "hailed with unusual pleasure" the fraternal

120. 12 Nov. 1839, AHMS.
121. MIS, *1*, 346–49.
122. MSP, OS, *3*, 133.

delegates from two New School presbyteries. They looked to a "harmonious and honorable blending of the two branches." In 1869 the presbytery vote for reunion was fifteen ayes to one nay. Ransom Hawley, the man who refrained from voting to divide the church back in 1838, was elected moderator of the reunited Presbytery of Indianapolis.[123] Those thirty years of separation in Indiana only proved how useless the division had been. The New School did not go radical after all, and the Congregationalists themselves abrogated the Plan of Union in 1852. The Old School and the New School developed nearly duplicate structures for administration and benevolent work. The records of the two church bodies are so similar that only an alert reader can tell if he is studying an Old School or a New School volume. The time until the reunion of the two denominations in 1870 seemed very long to most Indiana Presbyterians, and some communities did not wait.

The place of the Presbyterians in early Indiana was a very precarious one. Only a few of the more thriving places had congregations of enough size and vigor to do much building up of Zion. James Shields commented of Madison, Hamilton, and Delaware counties in 1835 that each had a small, struggling, and almost dead Presbyterian church. There were no Presbyterian ministers there, though they were wanted.[124] Destitution is the typical picture. The land was covered with presbyteries, but they were so weak and so short in ministerial members that the very cost of sending their commissioners to the General Assembly was a burden. This weakness was only made more grievous by division into Old School and New School.

John Dickey, in a letter to the American Home Missionary Society, stated that he believed it was utterly vain to think of supplying the West with a stated ministry in any reasonable length of time. He urged that the executive committee think

123. *History Indianapolis Presbytery* (Indianapolis, 1887), pp. 11–13.
124. Shields, Pendleton, letter to James H. Johnston, Madison, 15 Jan. 1835, AHMS.

realistically about the problem, because even if all the men in colleges and academies should in five years become ministers and come to the West, it would still be an inadequate supply.[125] Indiana was not an inviting field. The only hope was to make the best possible use of the men at hand. Some elaborate plans were made to widen the usefulness of ministers. Salem, La-Porte, and Indianapolis Presbyteries record detailed instructions for itineration.[126] In 1841 the Old School Synod of Indiana took stock of their "many destitutions" and "low state of religion." They advanced a plan by which every church with a pastor would allow him one-fifth of his time with pay to itinerate among churches without a minister.[127] The plan was a decided failure. Only one church in Indianapolis Presbytery would consent to have their minister spend one-fifth of his time on salary in missionary labors. Many of the churches expected their ministers to supply vacant churches occasionally but to use this as a sort of overtime work to bring their meager salary up to subsistence level. In all these plans two facts stand out: when the supply was hopelessly short, no plan of division was likely to make it ample; and in any event the Presbyterians did little more than pass a resounding resolution, declare a day of prayer and fasting, and then go home to do as they pleased. There was neither a "flinty-faced" executive, as Jeremiah Hill recommended, nor any presiding elder such as made the Methodist itineracy practicable.[128] Whenever the presbytery or synod took the trouble to check compliance on a directive or a recommendation, the report was usually disappointing.

The procedure for founding new churches was haphazard.

125. Clark County, 23 Jan. 1832, AHMS.
126. MSP, *1*, 132–35. Minutes of LaPorte Presbytery, *1*, 2. MIP, NS, *1*, 164; MIP, OS, *1*, 351.
127. MIS, OS, *1*, 90–92.
128. Hill, Spencer, 22 Aug. 1831, AHMS. William W. Sweet, "Early Methodist Circuits in Indiana," *IMH*, *10* (1914), 367–68. Francis I. Moats, "The Rise of Methodism in the Middle West," *MVHR*, *15* (1928), 78–79.

At first the missionaries and resident ministers simply constituted churches wherever they were able to gather a small group of members. The new church was enrolled by the presbytery and joined the chorus of those appealing for supply. Thus in 1831 James A. Carnahan "informed Presbytery that on the 14th day of May, he organized a church at Frankfort."[129] Later, some presbyteries required the permission of the presbytery prior to constituting any new church, although this was likely to be for partisan reasons. Eliphalet Kent had a congregation of fifteen or twenty ready to organize, but he feared Indianapolis Presbytery would not approve any new churches that were likely to be New School.[130] When these little churches were founded, they were often supervised so poorly that they died. Five of the earliest churches of Whitewater Presbytery were disbanded.[131] Such centers as Brookville and Salem had periods of deep depression in church life because of the lack of consistent leadership. S. A. Stewart compiled *A Presbyterial Graveyard* of disbanded churches for Logansport Presbytery. He aptly described the deaths as "without benefit of clergy, no friendly stated clerk to note the fact of their passing away. . . . The tale is told. No less than 25 churches, half our present number, have been pronounced dead by Presbytery."[132]

In 1850 the Old School and New School Presbyterians in Indiana reported exactly the same number of ministers; the New School had a small majority of churches, while the Old School had a small majority of members. Together the two branches accounted for 216 churches, 134 ministers, and 10,418 members. In that year the reported population of Indiana was 988,416. To use their own terms, the Presbyterians needed more ministers, more support for benevolent

129. Bessie L. Hufford, "One of Wabash College Founders," *Indianapolis Star*, 20 Nov. 1932.
130. Kent, Greenwood, 27 Feb. 1835, AHMS.
131. Maurice S. Lafuze, "Whitewater Presbytery: A Brief History" (mimeo, 1952), p. 1.
132. *Presbyterial Graveyard* (LaPorte, 1920), pp. 5–6, 10–11.

135

causes, and, if not a revival, at least some mercy drops from heaven.

Presbyterian congregations laid the foundations of the faith at many points in the West and had their peculiar contribution to make wherever they were gathered. When Isaac Reed constituted the church at Greenwood (then called Greenfield) on the last day of 1825, he made plain its context in Zion:

> God, in whose hands our times are, and whose are all our ways, in his Providence hath severed us from our brethren, our churches, and our ministers in yon land of our fathers' sepulchres, and hath set us down here. But this day is witness, and we ourselves are witnesses, that Jehovah's ways to us are full of mercy. For the church of Harodsburg and Providence, behold, he gives us a church in Greenfield. Scarcely is the wild man gone; scarcely is the wild beast fled, and the banner of the Lord is set up. . . .
>
> May we live as good citizens; may Christ be our foundation, and the gospel our guide and our hope; may we live as *Christians*,—and may the blessings of the Lord our God be upon us, and upon our children after us; and thus may Greenfield flourish.[133]

---

133. *Christian Traveller*, pp. 151–52.

CHAPTER FOUR ✠ THE TEACHING

Basic teaching in the Presbyterian Church is the Bible, the Westminster Confession of Faith, the Larger and Shorter Catechisms. This was the heart of the teaching material offered by the Presbyterians of early Indiana. Ministers expected to teach the Bible to the youth in Sabbath schools and to the adults in Bible classes. This was a standard item in missionary reports. It was thought to be of the utmost importance that the minister set up these classes and schools in the community where he, too, was considered a pioneer. The only duty of greater importance was that of organizing and caring for his new congregation.[1] It was easier to enlist the children than the adults. In the Sabbath school the scholars memorized considerable sections of the Bible by rote and perhaps by heart. However, adult settlers who would flock to camp meetings to participate in social and emotional exercises were more wary of systematic Bible study. Some were suspicious of this novel schooling advanced by educated preachers; more were afraid of revealing their ignorance.[2]

1. Frederick I. Kuhns, "Home Missions and Education in the Old Northwest," *JPHS, 31* (1953), 142.
2. Leander Cobb, Charlestown, 7 May 1828, AHMS.

The effort was unrelenting. When the American Bible Society resolved to supply the whole reading population of the world with the Bible, the Presbyterian pastor busied himself seeing that there was a Bible in every home in his county. The records show that either he was teaching a Bible class composed of a nucleus of the faithful, or he was about to gather such a group soon. It was the Bible class of the adults which furnished teachers for the Sabbath school for the young. Response was varied. Cressy packed in the town to hear his lectures on the authenticity of the Bible. More often the Bible study group was a handful of loyal members maintaining a sort of island of consistent study in a sea of revivalism. In the synod meetings it was urged that the presbyteries hire colporteurs to distribute Bibles and literature within their bounds. In almost typical fashion, the presbyteries set off on the venture with a resounding resolution and high hopes. Just as typically, the plan failed for lack of personnel, supervision, and support.[3] But determination to distribute and teach the Bible remained.

The Indiana frontier was maddening to the Presbyterian missionary. He was watched to ascertain his reaction to the Bible preaching of the folk religions. If he was silent, it was assumed he concurred in the backwoods exegesis. If he protested, he was charged with sectarianism and obstructing the Spirit. In his own sermons, at least, he could make the Bible teaching plain. And so he did. Monfort's sermon on justification begins with a first point of five pages, "What is the scriptural meaning of the term justification?" Caleb Mills begins his sermon on Malachi 3:8, "Will a Man Rob God," with a careful and typical biblical introduction. He outlines the situation to which Malachi spoke and then proceeds to the universal application of it to Gentiles as well. William W. Martin's sermon on I John 2:2 opens with a doxology and proceeds to an outline of the sermon points. Then comes a pause, "But before I proceed to show that Jesus Christ is a

3. MSP, *1*, 68–69. MIP, OS, *1*, 236–39, 263–64. MSP, OS, *1*, 167–69, 218. MSP, NS, *1*, 104, 116.

propitiatory sacrifice, I would briefly explain the term propitiation." There follows a three-page biblical word study complete with Greek. There is a beauty and symmetry and
accuracy about these sermons.[4] But there is little wonder that
the Hoosiers found them heavy going.

Catechisms were a major tool of Christian education. The
Assembly edited them and commended them to the churches;
the synod urged their use. The Shorter Catechism was the one
commonly used for young people. The 1848 resolution of the
Salem Presbytery, New School, quite typically stated that the
minister should catechize the children of their churches in the
Assembly's catechism and should be questioned at every
presbytery meeting about their performance of this duty.[5]
Ideally, the parents were to teach the catechism day by day.
On Sundays the minister was to assist in the teaching; and if
there was no minister, the elders were to attend to the catechizing. Missionaries in destitute areas were to catechize
children in their travels. Twice each year there was to be a
gathering of parents and children for recitation of catechism
and for counseling in family relations by the pastor. Considering the nature of the settlers and the number of churches without ministers, J.S. Armentrout's cautious statement was correct,
"When one recalls the emphasis placed by the General
Assembly upon the responsibility of the pastor for catechizing,
one can assume that wherever there was such a pastor some
Christian teaching was being done."[6]

The Westminster Confession is itself a highly developed
body of dogma, the longest creed in Christendom. Presbyterian ministers of the early nineteenth century often used this
Confession as a beginning point, and from it they developed
an even more minute system as the heart of their theological
education. John McMillan taught theology in his "log college"

4. David Monfort, *Sermon on Justification, from Romans 3:24*, Indianapolis,
    1831. Mills, Sept. 1837 (MS in Indiana State Library). Martin, Sept.
    1811 (MS in Indiana Synod Office), pp. 2–4.
5. MSP, NS, *1*, 189.
6. "Early Christian Education in Indiana," *McCormick Speaking*, *8* (1955), 7.

in southwestern Pennsylvania. His procedure was to read lectures arranged in the form of questions and answers. These the students transcribed and learned to recite word for word.[7] John Matthews, first professsor of theology at Indiana Theological Seminary in 1831, used the Confession of Faith as his sole textbook. The next professor of theology used some new methods, as one might expect of a man named Erasmus Darwin McMaster. He used no written lectures and perhaps no written sermons. Each student recited on the topic of the day after research in the Bible and other sources. However, the old system returned and persisted even after Indiana Seminary changed its location to Chicago and its name to the Seminary of the Northwest:

> The Seminary of the Northwest stuck with the Old School. After the publication of Hodge's Systematic Theology, 1871, Professor Thomas H. Skinner prepared a set of "Questions in the Theological Course of the Seminary of the Northwest." He had eleven hundred and two questions, based on Hodge and the Confession of Faith, for the three-year course in theology. In those days the Lord kept no secrets from his servants! Incredible as it may seem to us, theology had hardly any place for mystery in it. Man took possession of this world and also of the next.[8]

The detailed system of the Old School is well illustrated by the preaching of David Monfort of Franklin and William Martin of Livonia. It comes from the Bible, from the Confession —and also certainly from Princeton, which under the influence of President Witherspoon had been purged of the Edwards theology and had now become a centre of Scotch-Irish conservatism stoutly resisting the New Haven Theology of

7. William W. Sweet, "The Rise of Theological Schools in America," *CH, 6* (1937), 268.

8. Joseph Haroutunian, "Then and Now—in Theology," *McCormick Speaking, 8* (1955), 12.

Nathaniel W. Taylor.[9] Monfort studied at Princeton. In 1831, as pastor at Franklin, he published his *Sermon on Justification from Romans 3:24.* The mood is indicated in the center of the title page by the verse "Earnestly contend for the faith which was once delivered to the saints." At the very beginning he puts the whole body of mankind in sin and guilt without hope of redemption in their own right. There are three points to Monfort's sermon.

Point one demonstrates the scriptural meaning of the term justification. Justification, according to Monfort, is strictly a legal or forensic term—the antonym of the word "guilt." There follow three pages of exegesis and collation to show the meaning of guilt. When a man is guilty he stands justly charged with a crime and is bound to suffer the penalty of law. Whatever his delinquency, he is bound to the corresponding process of law and bound to render the fitting penal obedience. Man stands in sin and owes the penalty. But justification is precisely the opposite of guilt. "Guilt is obligation to punishment; justification is exemption from that state." The justified person is declared righteous and innocent and freed from penal sufferings. It is in these terms that the sinner who is justified is declared free from the guilt of sin because his debt has been blotted out, canceled, annihilated as if it never existed. This does not hinge upon or imply a change of his moral nature or qualities, though such a change comes to the justified. What is important to Monfort here is the change in the sinner's legal status. When God justifies him he is judicially a different and righteous person and entitled to the benefits due such a man. But God is true and righteous; He cannot say what is not true or do what is not right. Therefore he cannot, without sufficient legal cause, pronounce a guilty sinner righteous. Sufficient cause for this would have to be a very valuable consideration, indeed.

In his second point Monfort describes the medium of the sinner's justification, the sufficient cause which is the redemption that is in Christ Jesus. To redeem is to pay the price, or

9. Trinterud, *Forming American Tradition,* pp. 261–65.

valuable consideration, by which a person or thing is bought back. Redemption must offer something conforming to the claim owed in both nature and extent. Now what is the nature and extent of the claim against man the guilty and condemned sinner? The nature of the claim against man is blood—it is his life. The sinner deserves nothing other than to die, broken against the righteousness of the law. So it is that "without the shedding of blood there is no remission." Thus it is the blood of Christ which is our redemption price; it is his life. As to the extent of the claim, it is beyond language or computation. But here, too, the ransom is sufficient, for the Redeemer is without blemish and he is very God. This adequate Redeemer took the place of guilty man, sustained the penalty for him, and was released from the bonds of death as an evidence that his work was satisfactory.

At this point the language becomes crucial. Monfort discusses imputation, the application of the work of Christ to the sinner. He says that the Scriptures speak of God's "not imputing sin" and of his "imputing righteousness." He finds the same usage in the church standards. To impute is to reckon or account a thing with legal effect. So the righteousness of Christ imputed to us men for our justification affects our legal rather than our moral status. The sinner owes a debt and penalty which he can never pay but by imputation; the Redeemer as his surety takes his place, and this is set to the account of the sinner so that his situation is precisely the same as if he had never been guilty.

Point three is polemic against those who charge: if God insists upon a satisfaction so minute, then where is His grace? Monfort is rather at a loss here but stoutly affirms that his position is the scriptural one, "that the justification of the sinner is gracious and yet that a sinner is justified mediately, through a price being paid for his ransom which fully comes up to the claims of law."

In a four-page conclusion he repeats the substance of the sermon and lays a few more blows upon the "professedly orthodox." Then comes the invitation. It is a moving plea for sinners to come to the Saviour whose remedy is great enough for the need of the most desperate case. "Let us then come boldy to the throne of grace, pleading the merits of the surety; and from guilty and condemned rebels, we shall become the accepted and the adopted sons and daughters of the Lord Almighty. AMEN"[10]

As if to answer any critic who questioned why an expounder of limited atonement should offer a general invitation, Monfort adds an appendix. The argument it expounds offers an interesting insight into the appeal of New School doctrine: Some have been saying the atonement is sufficient for all men as if this were something new. There is nothing new about it. Old School men believe this. It is not right to taunt us as if "our atonement is just large enough for ourselves and a few of our favourite neighbors." The work of Christ might extend to all as simply and efficiently as membership in a nation extends to six million or twelve million. Old School preachers give an unrestricted invitation and offer of salvation to sinners because (1) they are commissioned to preach the gospel to every creature; (2) the provision is unlimited; (3) the provision is suitable to the situation of every kind of sinner; (4) offering the gospel to sinners is the means appointed for bringing them to Christ—by this means the Redeemer gathers his sheep. The offer is made to all who will accept; all who will accept are assured they will be saved. However, the atonement is sufficient for all; it is efficient in the elect. It is not right to say Christ died for all men. If this were true, either Christ was thwarted or men may be saved who never receive the gift of the Spirit. For this gift God bestows only upon some.

A closely penned manuscript of William W. Martin (September 1811) teaches the same system. The text is I John 2:2, "And he is the propitiation for our sins; and not for ours only but also for the sins of the whole world." Most of the sermon is spent reducing the scope of the text to true believers, the elect.

10. Pages 8–15, 20, 24–25.

He builds an overwhelming case. Then he proceeds to a moving general invitation! The doctrines of eternal election and of particular redemption are not to be a stumbling block to any. Since the decrees of God are secret they cannot be used by us as excuses for holding back. Martin cries out the great evangelistic texts of invitation: "Let the wicked forsake his way . . . He that cometh to me I will in no wise cast out. . . . Come unto me all ye that labor and are heavy laden . . . Let none through their unwillingness to be saved account themselves unworthy of everlasting life, for salvation is sovereign and free to whosoever will."[11]

New School men did not care for the mechanics of imputation. They believed that all men are themselves sinners without hope apart from the grace of God. Why the insistence that Adam's sin be imputed to all men? They believed that Christ's life and obedience unto death was sufficient to offer atonement and reconciliation to all men. But they rebelled, even in the face of the King James Version of Romans 4:4–11 and II Corinthians 5:19–21, at saying that the righteousness of Christ was imputed to some solely by God's decree. The passivity and impersonality of it offended them. To be sure, only some are saved, and these are the elect. No man saves himself by an act of his own. God calls him by name and he responds. But the very way in which God calls the elect is by the gift of the Spirit moving them to decision. God does not move men like stones or pawns. He so fires their wills that they will to respond. For this he uses means such as Sabbath schools, Bible classes, missionary sermons, even revivals with "anxious seats."

James R. Wheelock of Greensburg represented the more strenuous New School teaching in Indiana. He claimed to preach the entire and universal depravity of men but he told the people this was blameable depravity and the more there was of depravity the more there was of guilt. He said that men did not lose their capacities as moral agents in Adam, and that

11. Pages 25–30.

they now had all the powers and capacity necessary to comply with God's commands, for Jesus Christ is the propitiation for the sins of the whole world. Believers are active as they turn to Christ and repent under the influence of the Holy Spirit who convicts men of sin and makes them willing to do what they had power to do before but would not. Wheelock said this New England divinity not only squared with the Presbyterians' Confession of Faith, but would prove the very salvation of the Presbyterian Church.[12]

Wheelock had little patience with the Old School forces. It was Monfort and Sickels who marshaled enough Old School elders to control the Indianapolis Presbytery and turn that body against him. There was a "friendly conference" from candle-lighting to midnight and again for half the following day to see if the Old School and New School parties could "agree to walk together as brothers." Neither would yield enough on doctrine to allow compromise. When the question was put individually, "Can you forbear," the New School party would tolerate the Old but the Old School counted the New too dangerous to be allowed. They proceeded to trial.[13] Wheelock deplored the founding of his church at Greensburg; he felt he could have done better from scratch. In a report to the Society in 1833 he strongly stated his view that Lowry had organized the church too soon and of too heterogeneous a group. A few had letters from churches in Kentucky, a few from Pennsylvania but most members had no letters at all and no spirituality either. The influence here was Ultra Old School because of its southern members and ministers. Also, members of the Sand Creek church who had relatives at Greensburg were using the church organization to inflame their prejudice against New England men and the New Divinity. Had there as yet been no church at Greensburg, the Old School tactics would not have been so successful. Wheelock cried out for anything except the ignorant, self-righteous, Kentucky Presbyterianism

12. 27 Aug. 1832, AHMS.
13. Wheelock, 10 Jan. 1833, AHMS.

he had to tolerate. Most of the churches in his area reminded him of old houses whose owners could not decide whether to repair or simply to pull down and build all over again.[14]

Two years later Wheelock was at Clinton in the midst of a revival. His report to the Society gives another insight into New School preaching. He said the membership of the Clinton church had been brought to real heart searching by the Holy Spirit. For some time attendance at preaching had been good while he preached on man's entire alienation of heart from God, on salvation by grace alone in the atoning blood of Christ, on man's obligation to repent and believe, on man's dependence on the Holy Spirit to move him to repentance because of his voluntary opposition to God, and on the sufficiency of the atonement to meet the need of every sinner. "Christians were brought to feel that the greatest blessing we needed and almost the only one was the gift of the Holy Spirit. Some were brought to feel they could not endure the thought of living as they had done; that vain was the help of man."[15]

When Wheelock was tried before the Synod of Indiana, he was let go with admonishment on a vote which followed party lines, and he was advised to be more careful. Fourteen members of the synod promptly protested, listing what for them were the crucial points: "On the subject of federal representation, imputation, and the atonement of Christ, Mr. Wheelock does vary materially from the standards of our church; and moreover that this testimony was abundantly confirmed by Mr. Wheelock's written confession."[16]

There was also much variety within the New School group itself. Wheelock was full of New England Divinity besides being volatile and eccentric. James H. Johnston at Madison liked the New England way of formulating theology, but was more careful not to give offense. Johnston's funeral sermon for his schoolmate and friend, Albert Barnes, seemed to give

14. 9 May 1833, AHMS.
15. Clinton, 5 Feb. 1835, AHMS.
16. MIS, *1*, 156.

support to the views for which Barnes had been investigated by the Old School in Philadelphia.[17] Isaac Reed was a New School man whose view of election was limited enough to pass muster with the most watchful of the Old School; he affirmed his agreement with a letter of George Whitefield to John Wesley: "There was an eternal compact, between the Father and the Son. A certain number was then given him, as the purchase of his obedience and death. For these he prayed, John xvii and not for the world: for these and these only, he is now interceding; and with their salvation he will be fully satisfied."[18]

Theological giants of the Calvinist world wrestled with the doctrinal issues between Old School and New School from 1798 to 1870. Some were men of such stature that the historian desires to treat with respect the differences which exercised them so. But this is difficult to do; for, if there was indeed a clear issue in the days of Edwards and Hopkins, it seems to have lost its clarity before the engagements on the Hoosier frontier. Perhaps Elwyn Smith is right: "By the end of the century, perception of the theological problem had died out and the lines were drawn for an ecclesiastical schism almost wholly devoid of theological insight."[19] At any rate, one cannot help feeling that in Indiana much of the doctrinal difference between the Old School and the New School was only a playing with words. When a man becomes a Christian, is it because he makes the move or because the Spirit moves him without violation, through his own will, because God has decreed from all eternity that he was one for whom Christ died? Is it better to declare that the repentant sinner is freed from a complex slavery to sin and justified through Christ because of the great mercy and grace of God, or must it be said that the righteousness of Christ is divinely imputed to some even as the sin of Adam is legally imputed to all? These hardly look so

17. *The Dead Who Die in the Lord Are Blessed* (Philadelphia, 1874).
18. *Christian Traveller*, p. 53.
19. "The Doctrine of Imputation and the Presbyterian Schism of 1837–1838," *JPHS, 38* (1960), 149.

incompatible as to require division of a great church. The same doctrinal division was in the united church before 1830 and after 1870. This is the sort of dialogue one might expect between theological seminaries or within them. Apart from the Scotch-Irish resentment of Yankee culture and the struggle for ecclesiastical control of missions, these theological differences would not have precipitated division. However, in the heat of the struggle the Old School laid great stress on limited atonement, imputation, and the initiative of God. They made the Confession of Faith mean what their baroque system had deduced from it. On the other hand, the New School interpreted the Confession to "make sense"—that is, to fit with man's natural impression of freedom. They took liberties with the plain wording, especially in the matter of imputation. This came very near to opportunism at times. Lyman Beecher declared, "I knew to a hair's breadth every point between Old School and New School, and knew all their difficulties and how to puzzle them with them."[20]

Distinguishing the two in doctrine was a hair's breadth business. It was mostly a matter of specialized vocabulary, a difference of phraseology and mode of illustration. The three points of an Old School sermon might vary from those of a New School sermon if the sermon was on a controversial doctrine, but even then the conclusion and the invitation were the same. One looks in vain for libertine tendencies in the New School records. The catechisms and the Confession are respected and their use urged. Sabbath-breaking is condemned as stoutly as ever. There is no laxity in the examination of candidates. Elders are as much in attendance as in Old School bodies. The sermons are equally long and on the same topics. One New School presbytery even reprimands the official New School paper for being too Congregational and demands a mending of ways. The reader must learn to watch carefully for a limited number of check points to differentiate an Old School

20. Charles Beecher, ed., *Autobiography, Correspondence, etc. of Lyman Beecher* (2 vols. New York, 1864), 2, 187.

record book from a New School book after 1838.

At one unfortunate point the Presbyterian preachers in early Indiana were alike. They were too rationalistic for the settlers. They kept answering questions the frontiersmen were not asking. Both the Old School and the New School held and preached a theological system which was complex and mature. They were fascinated by the intricacies of total depravity, election, limited atonement, irresistible grace, and perseverance of the saints. They liked to preach on predestination, regeneration, and human ability. Even when the doctrine preached seemed inevitable and right, as much of it was, it continued to be graduate school material offered to kindergarten. There were not many Presbyterian preachers on the Indiana frontier, and few of those present were good communicators to the settlers. After the New Purchase men heard the preaching of Baynard Hall, one remarked. "Foo! I don't want no more sich! I like a man that kin jist read, and then I know it comes from the sperit! he tuk out his goold watch twice to show it, and was so d-mnation proud he wouldn't kneel down to pray!"[21] Most of the Presbyterians were faithful preachers; only a handful were popular.

The failure of Presbyterians to understand one another was pathetic. When the Synod of Indiana met at New Albany in 1834, it issued its solemn testimony against seven errors in doctrine.[22] Presumably these were to be errors of the New School. But the most radical New School men in the state would not have espoused this list. The New School men did not protest the syllabus of errors; they did not feel themselves affected by it.

Even more critical was the failure of non-Presbyterians to understand the Presbyterian theology. The system was offensive to Barton W. Stone. He never appreciated the contribution Calvinism made to his own life and theory, and he opposed it stoutly. Stone's aversion to creeds was particularly developed

21. *New Purchase*, p. 326.
22. MIS, *1*, 186–88.

in relation to the Presbyterians' Westminster Confession. His aversion to the doctrine of original sin was developed in relation to the Presbyterian James McGready, who was not orthodox on the subject of man's nature. Stone's chief loyalty was to revivalism, and his chief target was Calvinism, which he described as "among the heaviest clogs on Christianity in the world. It is a dark mountain between heaven and earth, and is amongst the most discouraging hindrances to sinners from seeking the Kingdom of God, and engenders bondage and gloominess to the saints. Its influence is felt throughout the Christian world, even where it is least suspected . . . yet there are thousands of precious saints in the system."[23] As the "New Lights" (Christian denomination) increased rapidly in Indiana, they carried distrust of Calvinism with them. It was common for the Methodists to caricature Calvinism and its tenets. Presbyterian doctrine of the church was battered by many who had no doctrine of the church and felt no need for one.[24] Moreover, since 1800 in America it has not been thought inconsistent that critics chide the Calvinists, although their own theology offers no alternative except a limited God. Baynard Hall's camp-meeting preacher is as profound as more recent alternatives: some things God just chose not to foreknow.[25]

The Presbyterians developed an impressive body of social teachings. It was their special concern to be building up Zion everywhere. In such matters as drinking, dancing, profanity, fighting, and Sabbath-breaking they disciplined their own members and tried their utmost to shape public opinion in the community. They deplored sexual looseness and labored to

23. William G. West, *Barton Warren Stone; Early American Advocate of Christian Unity* (Nashville, Disciples of Christ Historical Society, 1954) p. 108; see also pp. 8, 24, and chap. 6.
24. Hall, *New Purchase*, pp. 375-77; Robert H. Nichols, "The Influence of the American Environment on the Conception of the Church in American Protestantism," *CH, 11* (1942), 181-92.
25. *New Purchase*, p. 377.

strengthen healthy family relations. There were few idlers attending preaching, but there were many consumed with a hunger for wealth and a zeal for speculation. These the Presbyterians criticized. In the disastrous depression of 1818-19, the General Assembly spoke its mind saying that the times were the result of the spirit of cupidity, of adventurous and unjustifiable speculation, of extravagance and luxury, which prevailed in the land, as well as the want of that kind of education which is calculated to prepare youth for solid usefulness in the church and civil society. In his sermon entitled "Will a Man Rob God." Caleb Mills said that the misimprovement of time was robbery but so was the misuse of influence and wealth.[26]

Of all social issues, slavery was uppermost. In 1818 the Presbyterian General Assembly took a most vigorous stand against it. The statement was written by Ashbel Green, Baxter, and Burgess, and unanimously adopted. Slavery was ruled out on grounds of natural rights and of the gospel. No time was to be wasted: the slaves were to be educated, evangelized, and freed without delay. Sessions and presbyteries were to take action against violators.[27] This action was never rescinded. However, as cotton culture grew more profitable after the widespread use of the cotton gin and as the abolition societies moved from the South to the North, the Presbyterian statements on slavery became fewer and more tolerant. The Old School party was especially cautious and left room in the church for those who flatly stated that slavery was ordained of God.

Not so in Indiana. All the church bodies appear to have been strongly antislavery from the beginning. At its first meeting the Synod of Indiana prepared an eleven-page memorial on the subject of "African slavery." They quoted to the Assembly its own action of 1818 and called for action:

26. 27 Sept. 1837 (MS in Indiana State Library).
27. *Testimony of the General Assembly of the Presbyterian Church in the United States of America on the Subject of Slavery* (Philadelphia, 1858), p. 10.

But is it not high time, seeing the evil is one of such enormity—outraging "the most precious and sacred rights of human nature, being utterly inconsistent with the law of God, and totally irreconcilable with the principles and spirit of the gospel of Christ,"— is it not high time, we say, to enquire whether those concerned have manifested a disposition to obey them that have the rule over them, and watch for souls, as they that must give account? Have they taught their slaves to read the word of God, and brought them up as their own children, "in the nurture and admonition of the Lord?" And have they, as their slaves, become prepared, under the fostering hand of Christian benevolence, "unloosed the heavy burden and let the oppressed go free?" Nothing of all this. When we cast our eyes over the abodes of slavery, the same appalling spectacle is every where presented that called for the monitory voice of the Assembly. The same ignorance, the same vicious habits, together with a fearful augmentation of their numbers.[28]

As for the Colonization Society plan to return the Negroes to Africa, this was being used to forestall the only action that was right—abolition.

From that time on, the resolutions became even more pressing. The Indiana presbyteries and synods heaped invective upon slavery and finally upon slaveholders.[29] The New School Presbyterian Church had little constituency in the South and took a consistently antislavery stand. But that was not strong enough for the New School in Indiana. In 1838 the Synod of Indiana, New School, said the influence of slavery was largely responsible for the division of the church and quoted the Assembly of 1818 with the added sentiment, "It follows that the church ought to take speedy and decisive measures to

28. MIS, *1*, 22–23.

29. Ibid., pp. 145, 257–59, 311–20, 335, 351–57. MSP, *1*, 328–32. MIP, *1*, 238–39. MIP, NS, *1*, 23, 167–70. MLP, *1*, 84–85, 152.

purify itself from this long continued and enormous evil."[30] By 1843 this synod could address a special synodical letter of ten pages to the ministers and members of the slaveholding states.[31] They affirmed their love of the southern brethren and their own good motives, but they left both slavery and slaveholders entirely without excuse. The next year the synod resolved to inform the New School Assembly of its regret at the soft handling of the sin of slaveholding.

The Old School Presbyterians in Indiana were more quiet about slavery but quite capable of embarrassing the national church which was trying to hedge on the subject. Lake Presbytery prepared a memorial to the Old School Assembly commending the worthy stand taken by the Assembly of 1818 and urging that no retraction whatever be made from such a position.[32] Old School bodies like the Synod of Indiana and the Synod of Northern Indiana strengthened Lincoln's hand in proclaiming emancipation.[33]

It was easy for Indiana Presbyterians to condemn slavery, because there were so few slaves in the state. Buley stated that at the time of the indenture law of 1810 there were 237 slaves listed in Indiana, and active slavery agitation stopped there. Slavery remained a political issue, however, until long after statehood.[34] Condemnation of slavery passed all too quickly into condemnation of slaveholders and the denial that a slaveholder could be Christian. An example of antislavery polemic is the treatise of the Presbyterian minister James Duncan at Vevay. In eighty-eight tightly printed pages Duncan shows slavery squarely opposed to natural rights, to moral law, to all ten commandments in turn, to republican principles, to the church, and to the scriptures of both the Old and New Testaments. He includes such gems as "The Slaveholders Prayer"

30. MIS, NS, p. 259.
31. Ibid., pp. 311–20.
32. MLP, *1*, 152.
33. Lewis G. Vander Velde, *The Presbyterian Churches and the Federal Union 1861–1869* (Cambridge, Harvard University Press, 1932), pp. 117–18.
34. Buley, *Old Northwest*, *2*, 6.

and "Soliloquy for a Dying Slaveholder." In the center of the title page appears the quatrain:

> Columbia speak, let SLAVERY'S dirge be sung
> Wide o'er the world, the joyful sound begun;
> Shall bid the age of crime and suffring cease,
> And hail the dawn of freedom and of peace.[35]

There were many Hoosiers in the Presbyterian party which required abject repentance and elaborate loyalty oaths of all slaveholders after the War between the States. This was the sort of zeal which caused many border-state churches to secede after the war to join the Southern Assembly.[36] |The southern settlers in Indiana were largely upland settlers and not from the plantation economy. Many of Indiana's citizens had moved there for the very purpose of escaping the slave culture. Neither the Scotch-Irish, back-country man nor the Yankee missionary had any love for slavery. There was little struggle among Indiana Presbyterians over this issue; they were generally agreed against it.

Polemic was not limited to the slaveholder. Presbyterian preachers were always doing battle with the infidel. In 1830 Samuel Alexander declared:

> Infidelity is becoming consolidated in Vincennes. Thomas Payn and Ecce Homo are industriously circulated here. There are thirty six subscribers here for a periodical published in your city entitled *Priest-craft Unmasked;* if you have anything to meet this work, please send it to us immediately; for infidels are doing all they can against religion, but I and God's people here are not discouraged for his promise is that "no weapon formed against Zion shall prosper." Last

---

35. James Duncan, *A Treatise on Slavery in Which Is Shown Forth the Evil of Slave Holding Both from the Light of Nature and Divine Revelation* (Vevay, 1824), 88 pp.
36. Vander Velde, pp. 183–216.

month after much preparation previously there was an appointment for forming a county Temperance Society. We met and infidels, distillers, venders, drinkers and drunkards met and opposed us in every measure, to the surprise of all the sober thinking part of the community, but notwithstanding the opposition we formed a society numbering seventy members and have the prospect of many more. The good cause is certainly advancing. One of the leaders of the infidel band was asked to subscribe for my support, and in reply said that he would give something hansome if I would leave the place.[37]

Alexander was not alone in his difficulties; however, most Presbyterian missionaries were faced with the same discouraging situation at that time. Another typical report, also written in 1830, came from Benjamin C. Cressy of Salem:

When I arrived at this place and became acquainted with the distracted state of the church, I felt a sinking of spirits, and had melancholly apprehensions in view of my future prospects. It is generally acknowledged by those capable of judging that this village contains more infidels, and influential opposers of religion than any other place in the State of the same population. Sabbath breaking, intemperance, profanity and their attendant vices, have, and continue to prevail to an alarming extent. With preaching but occasionally, and while many were exclaiming, relative to this church, *"raze it, raze it* to the foundations" God's people had in a measure become disheartened in view of abounding iniquity. As the church was divided among themselves and being severely persecuted by those from without, I felt deeply impressed that our only hope was in him who can bring good out of evil and order out of confusion.[38]

37. Vincennes, 12 Jan. 1830, AHMS.   38. 7 June 1830, AHMS.

Historical evidence makes plain that from the early days there was a virulent strain of infidelity in Kentucky.[39] Some of this would have naturally moved into Indiana. However, the missionaries seemed prone to use the term "infidel" quite loosely to refer to opponents or to noncooperators in their program. Wherever an active infidel appeared, he got a lot of coverage for the reports back East.[40] He might be an educated nonconformist, a sort of professional protestant of irreligion, or he might be a bumptious frontiersman with no evident motive beyond troubling the preacher and getting attention for himself. One of the latter advanced three propositions to the Rev. Moody Chase at Danville: (1) there is no difference between the Protestant and Catholic priests; (2) the Protestants have always been a persecuting people; (3) Christians were the cause of the bloody revolution in France. The defense of the countryman was impregnable. He claimed to have read all literature on these subjects, especially any that was cited in rebuttal. He categorically denied the validity of any quotation against his position. If driven to get specific about any of his reading or claims, he answered all queries by stating that he was not obliged to tell. With that technique Chase reports, the skeptic emerged "wiser than seven men that can render a reason. . . . I mentioned this as a specimen of the character of infidels in this country, of their ignorance and positiveness. There are exceptions, but in the general this is true as far as my acquaintance extends."[41]

Still more troublesome to the Indiana Presbyterians were the activities of the Roman Catholics. Prior to the direct immigrations of the Irish and Germans there were only a handful of Catholics in the state. Buley judged that there were twenty thousand Catholics in Indiana in 1834. The new see of

39. Sweet, *Religion in American Culture*, pp. 211–15. Niels H. Sonne, *Liberal Kentucky, 1780–1828* (New York, Columbia University, 1939). Robert Davidson, *Presbyterian Church in Kentucky*, pp. 63–64, 99–103.

40. See Martin E. Marty, "The Uses of Infidelity," dissertation, University of Chicago, 1956.

41. Danville, 8 Dec. 1837, AHMS.

Vincennes included Indiana and eastern Illinois. Catholicism had not developed in the Northwest by the middle 1830s to a sufficient extent to explain the outburst of violent anti-Catholic sentiment, unless, perhaps, the people in the East were more agitated about the Pope's possible influence in the Mississippi Valley than were the Westerners themselves.[42] Presbyterians knew the candid authority claims of Rome well enough to be alarmed when that church structure and program followed the Catholic immigrants into Indiana. Their concern was well grounded, but their tactics for dealing with the situation often lacked both grace and effectiveness. A standard missionary remark upon surveying a new and needy field was that this would become a flourishing place, "Protestant or Catholic." The rather obvious aim of the remark was motivation to increase the missionary contributions back East.

Catholics were early involved in education, and this was an especially sore point with Presbyterians. Lyman Beecher's charge that Catholics were offering free education to Protestant children is echoed by Benjamin C. Cressy:

> In nine cases out of ten the children have returned home bigoted Catholics, and of this the Jesuits have made their boast. . . . The Catholic Priests in the Western Valley hesitate not to say to Protestant ministers: "You have come too late—we have already preoccupied the ground: if you intended to have done any thing you should have been here twenty years ago!" Equally arrogant is the language of the Bishop of Cincinnati who, in writing to his Catholic friends in Europe, remarks to this effect: "Our cause triumphs gloriously in America, and especially in the Mississippi Valley. We are looking forward with cheerful anticipations to the day *when all these heretics shall be embraced in the arms of the mother church!*" The Catholics in this country and Europe know full well

42. *Old Northwest*, 2, 471–72. For a concise summary of attacks on the Catholics see pp. 472–73.

that the great valley is destined to rule the United
States and no effort will be spared on their part to
be able ere long to rule the valley themselves.[43]

This kind of charge from several missionaries in Indiana led
the Synod of Indiana to resolve in 1831 that it should be considered highly improper for members of the Presbyterian
Church to entrust their children's education to Catholic
teachers. It was also recommended that the presbyteries
inquire of their churches concerning such an unwise practice
and take whatever measures were necessary to prevent Presbyterian children from being sent to Roman Catholic schools.[44]
During the next two years the synod's committee on Catholicism continued its investigation and report. A program to
inform Presbyterians about Catholicism was adopted. The
synod's resolution concerning academies for girls noted the
Catholic efforts in education and regretted that the Protestant
part of the community had done little or nothing to further
learning among young women. It was decided, therefore, that
ministers, elders, and all church members should be urged to
establish girl's schools as soon as possible and to make every
reasonable sacrifice to educate their daughters in these Protestant institutions. In this way, the temptation of parents to
send their girls to Catholic schools, thereby endangering their
minds and hearts, would be effectively avoided.[45] At least this
was what the synod had in mind.

In typical fashion, however, little was done about the synod's
resolutions. A few academies for girls were founded. A goodly
number of sermons were preached about the Catholic menace.
The Roman Catholic Church kept following its new constituency, winning very few non-Catholics but growing rapidly
by immigration. It is almost impossible to tell if concern about

43. Cressy, *Appeal for Indiana Seminary*, pp. 13–14. Elizabeth Denehie,
    "Catholic Education in Indiana; Past and Present," *IMH, 12* (1916),
    p. 339.
44. MIS, *1*, 118.
45. Ibid., p. 137.

Catholicism was significant in motivating Presbyterians on the frontier. One suspects that the polemic carried on by both sides accomplished little or nothing.

Every student of frontier history has noted the early leadership of Presbyterians and Congregationalists in education. Even a writer like Iglehart, who finds Presbyterian preachers on the frontier a sort of people without excuse, has a kind word to say about their relation to education:

> It cannot be denied that among the backwoodsmen who just settled Indiana there was much illiteracy, and that both secular and religious education was greatly to be desired. However such results may have been obtained, and making due allowance for the weakness of human nature under the circumstances, it must be admitted that the stand taken by the Presbyterians, both in matters of secular education and in the demand for an educated ministry, have in a substantial degree aided in the elevation of those standards and to that extent they are entitled to credit.[46]

Indiana's early settlers needed elementary education. Those few who had come directly from Massachusetts and Connecticut were the best trained, since they had not been a generation or two out of reach of the district school. But the bulk of Indiana immigrants, having come from the South, had been dependent on private schools, if indeed there had been any school available at all. People from the Middle Atlantic states were somewhere between, depending on the length of time they had tarried in the western country of New York, Pennsylvania, or Virginia.[47] The Presbyterian preachers were men with a double motivation to found schools: they saw the need for schools; they needed whatever meager financial support they could get by teaching. Five of the first Presbyterian minis-

46. "Methodism in Southwestern Indiana," *IMH, 17,* 138.
47. Buley, *Old Northwest, 2,* 330–31.

ters to settle in the state operated schools.[48] These were private classes that fitted a curriculum to the present status of the
student and pressed forward as far as circumstances allowed.
None of the admonitions of the American Home Missionary
Society were enough to get the preachers out of the schoolroom.
Lucius Alden and John Todd are examples of clergymen who
were incurable schoolmasters. At the age of sixty-three, when
his faculties had already failed somewhat and his preaching
had gone "a little wild," Todd went as a mission preacher to
the woods of Johnson County. His health was quite poor, but
he undertook the organization and care of common-school
classes for young women. These he offered free of charge. Later
he offered instruction to young men as well because he found
no qualified teachers in the vicinity. At first very few responded,
but then Todd wrote that the improvement shown by the
original pupils was attracting an increased enrollment. He was
hopeful that he would soon have them all reading and writing.[49]
It was Todd's school that the Wishard boys attended, five sons
of a Scotch-Irish farmer who had no zeal for higher education
for his family. William Henry Wishard and Joseph Milton
Wishard went on from that school to become physicians.
Samuel Ellis Wishard became a minister. James Harvey
Wishard became a newspaper editor. John Oliver Wishard did
not finish college and became a farmer; his four sons later
served as missionaries of the Presbyterian Church. Thus, in
just one instance, a bit of the influence of a preacher's school
can be traced. Todd was not simply pedagogue; he was pastor
in his school. He wrote a letter to William Henry Wishard
laying before him the urgency of professing his faith. "There
can be no discharge from the obligation. God has laid it upon
you. We have no command to bring you forcibly into the
church, but we would be guilty not to pass this law of God
upon you. . . . May the Lord direct you. You will receive this
as tendered from a sense of duty and with the sincerest regards

48. They were Samuel Scott, John M. Dickey, William Robinson, John
Todd, and William Martin.   49. 2 April 1835, AHMS.

to your interest in time and eternity."[50] Young Wishard professed his faith, united with the church at Greenwood, served seventy years as an elder, and attended six General Assemblies as commissioner of his presbytery.

The problems of the schoolmaster were not unrelated to those of the pastor. The same settlers who did not pay their subscription to the church did not pay their tuition to the school. Isaac Reed sent his daughter to Bedford, Pennsylvania, to study in her uncle's school there. After one year the sixteen-year-old Mary sent back some advice to her father, who was about to relocate:

> Dear papa, go somewhere where the people are able to pay for their education; teach *all* the languages, and keep a school of a high order. Have the tuition bills paid in advance; and admit none but those who will do it. Obtain some student who can teach the mathematics and languages;—mama could take charge of the female department till I return to you. Go where you can be the supply of a church, as uncle is here. Could you receive four or six hundred dollars a year for that, together with what the school brought in, would enable us to live in comfort and respectability. Begin with only ten scholars and they will increase. Have an exhibition—publish rules of the school, and get persons interested—take pains to have who is known. Keep boarders, and have high prices, after a while the people will be just as willing to pay them as low ones. If you cannot get others, take two rooms in the house in which you live, and have them fixed up for schoolrooms, and have exhibitions in the church. Have the girls read at the exhibition, and the boys speak, etc. I hope you will soon be comfortably situated.[51]

Mary came home sick, and died before she could help her

50. Wishard, *William Henry Wishard*, pp. 41, 78–83.
51. Isaac Reed, *Youth's Book* (Indianapolis, 1840), p. 96.

father with a school. Her father never found the place where he could take her advice.

Sabbath schools represent an attempt to widen the benefits of both education and religion. W. W. Sweet wrote that the Methodists seemed to have been the first to introduce Sunday schools into the United States as early as 1786, but that the movement had already gained considerable impetus in England before that date.[52] In Indiana the movement was inter-denominational from the start; the leadership was strongly Presbyterian. When Isaac Reed founded a Sabbath school in New Albany in 1818, he recorded that so far as he knew it was the first in the state. W. H. Levering says that his research has not authenticated an earlier one.[53] Indianapolis organized such a school in 1823, the year preceding the formation of the American Sunday School Union. This was probably the most influential Sabbath school in the state. It was a union or inter-denominational school for its first five years. However, it began from the Bible class of a Presbyterian elder, Isaac Coe, and was held in the carpenter shop of another elder, Caleb Scudder. The first report of the Indiana Sabbath School Union in 1827 shows that organization almost entirely in the hands of Presbyterians. Small wonder that some at first feared that the Sunday School movement was a channel for Presbyterian aggression. That fear was groundless. By the time of Indiana's first Sunday School convention in 1857, the Methodists had sixty-five schools represented, the Presbyterians thirty-seven, and the Baptists fourteen. There were representatives from twenty-three union schools.[54]

Perhaps the Indianapolis school will illustrate both the aim and operation of the movement. *The Indianapolis Gazette* for 5 April 1823 carried the notice, "The Indianapolis Sabbath School will commence next Sabbath, April 6th, at nine

52. *Story of Religion*, p. 367.
53. *Christian Traveller*, p. 89. Levering, *Historical Sketches of Sunday School Work in Indiana, North America, and beyond the Seas* (Lafayette, 1906), p. 8.
54. George S. Cottman, "Indiana's First Sunday-School Convention," *IMH, 6* (1910), 89.

o'clock in the morning, at Mr. Caleb Scudder's shop. A general and punctual attendance of scholars is requested, and that they should bring with them the Testaments Spelling Books, or such school books as they may have."[55] That first meeting had about thirty scholars but in three weeks attendance had increased to seventy. A system of rewards was introduced from the beginning. Money credit accrued to the scholar at the rate of one cent per verse of scripture memorized, ten verses read, or ten words spelled. The pupil's study books were then charged against him and any balance was payable in religious books. The amount of credit accrued determined the price level of the books the scholar was permitted to borrow from the library. A definite penalty scale was set up for damage of library books, the penalty to be taken from the scholar's credit or paid in cash or memory work. By 1836 a program of monthly visiting was in operation and more than three-fourths of the city's children were finally enrolled. On the Fourth of July the Superintendent, James Blake, marched his young army to hear the Declaration of Independence and eat gingerbread in the state-house square. Said one of the original members of the school:

> Fifty years ago to-day I entered that school, a boy eight years old, and did not know one letter of the alphabet, nor do I believe that among the ten or twelve boys present there was one who could spell his own name, or would know it should he see it in print. the incidents of that day were calculated to make a lasting impression on the young mind. The Sunday-school had been the topic of conversation with the boys of the village for some time. We thought it a great innovation upon our personal rights. We thought that Messrs. Coe, Blake, and Ray, who organized the school, were assuming power they had no right to. I was assigned to the class of the late James Blake, who taught me the alphabet, as well as to spell and

55. *Centennial First Church, Indianapolis*, p. 214.

read. In Mr. Blake's class I learned to repeat the Catechism, Lord's Prayer, and Ten Commandments. I remained in that school some nine or ten years and there
learned many useful and instructive lessons. The rules
at first were most rigid, and delinquency on the part of
the scholars was severely reprimanded and reported
to their parents. One of the rules required that we
should attend church on the Sabbath; hence Sunday
was a day of rest to the ground squirrels and rabbits.
Birds were left uninterrupted to build their nests. [56]

An interdenominational committee from Indianapolis organized some twenty schools in Marion, Hendricks, and Morgan
Counties. All the eastern missionaries who came West after
the founding of the American Sunday School Union in 1824
were fired with zeal for Sabbath schools. This was only increased when the American Sunday School Union began its
deliberate program to establish a Sabbath school in every
town in the West. The Synod of Indiana did its bit with a
resolution recommending that all pastors and sessions encourage the project and support it by asking their churches for
prayers and contributions in its behalf. [57] This meant that agents
of the American Sunday School Union must travel to organize
and inspire local leaders. It meant that every adult Bible class
became a training ground for teachers and sponsors. It also
meant that a lot of schools were poorly started and poorly run
so that they had to be started again and again.

It is easy to criticize the Sabbath schools. Their main business was memorization of the Bible, the catechism, and the
hymnal. Children were to be grouped in sections of six or
eight at the same learning level to progress through four stages
of schooling. The class began with a primer containing the
alphabet and words of one syllable. The next step was mastery
of a spelling book with words of two or more syllables. Then

56. Ibid., pp. 209, 214, 220, 233. Letter of J. H. B. Nowland, cited in Edson,
Early Indiana Presbyterians, p. 144.
57. MIS, *1*, 86.

the scholars were ready for stage three, the memorizing of catechisms and hymns. Those published by the American Sunday School Union were to˙be preferred since they were prepared by a committee representing the principal denominations and so were screened to exclude peculiar or offensive doctrines. "In the Indianapolis school, Watts' First Catechism, Milk for Babes, Watts' Divine and Moral Songs, Dodridge's Poetical Lessons, and Taylor's Original Hymns are learned in course, before commencing the Testament." Finally came the systematic mastery of Bible verses beginning with the second chapter of Matthew and continuing in John, Acts, and Romans. The entire Bible now became the text, but Old Testament passages were carefully selected at first.[58] However, the instructions to teachers made it plain that pupils were to be able to answer catechism questions "in different words" to ensure some understanding. The class studying the commandments was to hear the substance of the commandment in a few words from the teacher. There was to be more than mere rote.

Advocates of the Sabbath school made claims too stoutly and so incurred criticism. According to Buley, the claims that Sunday schools provided schooling as effective as that of day schools were detrimental to the efforts to provide really effective education.[59] Some zealots deserved the criticism; Sabbath schools in the place of a public school system would have been "little pious frauds." But opposition to public schools was certainly not the mood of the first report of the Indiana Sabbath School Union. "Let Sabbath Schools be established wherever it is practicable. They will answer the double purpose of paving the way for common schools, and of serving as a substitute till they are generally formed. Parents and children, becoming sensible to the sweets and the benefits of learning, will unite in one loud and determined call for the permanent means of education."[60] Sabbath schools were a makeshift.

58. *First Annual Report of the Indiana Sabbath School Union* (Indianapolis, 1827), pp. 8, 20.
59. *Old Northwest*, 2, 347.   60. *Sabbath School Union*, p. 12.

They taught some to read who would not otherwise have learned. They gave the new readers some material not unworthy. When one remembers that the sum of Lincoln's formal schooling was the most basic reading and writing, it seems wise to moderate criticism of a system which taught as much as this.

The private schools and the Sunday schools were reaching only a handful of the youth of Indiana and in most cases doing that inadequately. The need was for a public school system. In theory, Indiana was making good progress toward such a system; in fact, she was making little progress at all. The Ordinance of 1787 stated: "Religion, morality and knowledge being necessary to good government and the happiness of mankind, Schools and the means of education shall be forever encouraged," but that hardly established a school system. In practice it was no more effective than the next pronouncement in the ordinance, which stated that utmost good faith would always be observed toward the Indians. Indiana was the first state to make constitutional provision for a general system of education ascending in regular gradation from township schools to a state university which would be tuition free and equally open to all. The federal enabling act allowing the people of Indiana to form a state government had provided that the section of land numbered sixteen in every township was granted to the inhabitants for the use of schools. Further, one entire township was to be designated by the President for a state "seminary of learning."

Still, there was no school system for a generation. There were specific acts of the state legislature beginning in 1816, but the result was always that local people did entirely as they pleased. Each district had the power to decide whether to have a school or not, and only those patronizing the school felt liable for support. A law passed in 1836 allowed a householder to engage his own teacher and still draw his share of the state funds. Later the requirement of a teaching certificate was made optional within each district, and private and church schools were permitted to draw money from the public funds. Decentralization had reached an extreme.[61] Even fourteen years after Indiana's public school system was put on the statute books, very little money was spent for education. The legislature seemed powerless to enforce its own laws. The few schools that had been established often were ruled by ignorance and indifference. More laws were passed; the system failed to improve. There was no effective school organization, and the amount of illiteracy was alarming.[62]

Where there was a district school organized, good teachers were the exception rather than the rule:

> Teachers quite often in those days went on the hunt for their schools. They were a kind of tramp— homeless fellows, who went from place to place hunting for a job. When the prospect seemed good the candidate would write an "article of agreement," wherein he would propose to teach a quarter's school at so much per scholar. With that in hand he tramped the neighborhood over, soliciting subscribers, and, if a stranger, usually meeting with more scorn than goodwill. He was too often esteemed a good-for-nothing who was too lazy to work. . . . The only requirements were that the teachers should be able to teach reading, writing and ciphering. The teacher who could cipher all the sums in Pike's arithmetic, up to and including the rule of three, was considered a mathematician of no mean ability.[63]

Until the adoption of the new constitution in 1852, each school district had three trustees empowered to examine and certify teachers. This was somewhat limited by the fact that many of the trustees were illiterate. Scarcely one in a hundred was well enough educated to conduct a school, and yet these men

61. Paul Monroe, *Founding of the American Public School System: A History of Education in the United States* (New York, Macmillan, 1940), p. 291.
62. Richard G. Boone, *A History of Education in Indiana* (New York, 1892), pp. 38–39.
63. Banta, "The Early Schools of Indiana," p. 85.

examined the candidates for the teaching profession. So few of the trustees could read that the candidates' handwriting became an important factor, because it could be seen and judged by the uneducated without comment. Anyone who had a smooth, round, full hand was considered fit to teach in the district schools.[64] Edward Eggleston portrays the truth in his novel when he has his Hoosier schoolmaster meet the trustee:

> "You see," continued Mr. Means, spitting in a meditative sort of way, "you see, we a'n't none of your saft sort in these diggin's. It takes a *man* to boss this deestrick. Howsumdever, ef you think you kin trust your hide in Flat Crick school-house I ha'n't got no 'bjection. But ef you git licked, don't come on us. Flat Crick don't pay no 'nsurance, you bet! Any other trustees? Wal, yes. But as I pay the most taxes, t'others jist let me run the thing. You can begin right off a Monday. They a'n't been no other applications. You see, it takes grit to apply for this school. The last master had a black eye for a month. But, as I wuz sayin', you can jist roll up and wade in. I 'low you've got spunk, maybe, and that goes for a heap sight more'n sinnoo with boys. Walk in, and stay over Sunday with me. You'll hev' to board roun', and I guess you better begin here."[65]

The only hope seemed to lie in some effective centralized leadership and control. This would have to be done in the face of vigorous opposition. State education was feared as dangerous and undemocratic. A member of the state legislature declared in 1837, "When I die I want my epitaph written, 'Here lies an enemy to free schools'."[66] Caleb Mills was the Yankee Presbyterian preacher who deliberately set out as a one-man lobby for effective public schools.

64. William F. Vogel, "Home Life in Early Indiana," *IMH*, *10* (1914), 299.
65. *The Hoosier School-Master* (New York, Grosset and Dunlap, 1899), pp. 11–12. 66. Boone, p. 87.

It was not a new thing for missionaries to promote the cause of free public schools. Michigan, Illinois, and Indiana depended much upon preachers from the American Home Missionary Society to get their school system in operation.[67] The Yankee missionaries had known the "common schools" of the East; Connecticut, New Hampshire, and Massachusetts were at the top of the literacy list in 1840.[68] Caleb Mills was born in New Hampshire, and he was educated at Dartmouth College in New Hampshire and at Andover Seminary in Massachusetts. There is something wonderfully deliberate about Mills. After his first year of seminary he served two years as a Sunday School agent in Kentucky and Indiana and determined to settle in the Wabash Valley. Back at the seminary he laid plans for a common-school campaign for Indiana. He felt strongly that what the state needed was preaching of the Gospel and a system of public schools. Sabbath schools such as he had been organizing were good, but they were simply not sufficient for educating the masses:

> My thoughts have been directed of late to the subject of common-schools, and the best means of awakening a more lively interest in their establishment in the Western country. Public sentiment must be changed in regard to free schools; prejudice must be overcome, and the public mind awakened to the importance of carrying the means of education to every door. Though it is the work of years, yet it must and can be done. The sooner we embark in this enterprise, the better. It can be effected only by convincing the mass of the people that the scheme we propose is practicable; is the best and most economical way of giving their children an education. Introductory to, and in connection with these efforts, we must furnish them with teachers of a higher order of intellectual culture than the present race of pedagogues.[69]

67. Goodykoontz, *Home Missions*, pp. 367–69.
68. Boone, p. 88.   69. Moores, *Caleb Mills*, pp. 382–83.

Mills came to Crawfordsville to preach the Gospel as a Presbyterian missionary and to train teachers for the common schools by organizing the first classes at Wabash College in 1833.

In 1846 he began his personal campaign for free public schools. Evidently he felt that the situation was so bad that simply facing the facts would be motivation enough. In his study of Mills and the schools, Charles Moores commented on the situation:

> It is common tradition that until after the adoption of our modern school system in 1852 the name Hoosier was the synonym for ignorance. In 1790, Gen. Arthur St. Clair, then governor of the Northwest Territory, said of our pioneers, "They are the most ignorant people in the world. There is not a fiftieth man that can either read or write." In 1840, one-seventh of the entire grown population was illiterate, and Indiana stood lowest in intelligence of all the free states. In 1850, the proportion of illiterates had grown to one in every five, and Indiana had fallen below many slave states. Meanwhile, the proportion in Ohio was one in eighteen, and in Michigan, one in forty-four. In Indianapolis the first free public school was not opened until 1853.[70]

This was the situation Mills presented for consideration by the legislature. On the opening day of the sessions of 1846–51, he printed the facts in a series of papers published in the *Indiana State Journal* and signed "One of the People." Of the first paper Moores says, "It is a noble message, packed with startling facts, spiced with humor, and everywhere grand with common sense." The legislators read the messages. They were informed that "the true glory of a people consists in the intelligence and virtue of its individual members, and no more important duty can devolve upon its representatives in their legislative capacity than the devising and perfecting a wise,

70. Ibid., p. 363.

liberal, and efficient system of public education." Mills pointed out that in the present situation the representatives from Jackson, Martin, Clay, and Dubois counties could be much relieved of sending home newspapers and documents. Literally half of their constituents could not read them anyway. Ohio and Michigan had levied a tax in support of free public schools, and Mills expostulated: "What a contrast to the amount Indiana raised on the same principle! Shall it be stated? Will not the very announcement of it overwhelm the community and call forth a general outburst of indignation upon the legislature that has the hardihood to impose such enormous burdens for such an unimportant object? I will state it in *round* numbers, $0.000.0."[71] He advocated getting a good school system by paying for it and supervising it. His position was taken up by the newspapers and a host of friends of education. In 1848 the matter was put to the vote of the people. Opponents of the free schools charged that priestcraft and the connivings of the clergy were at work. The cry of church and state was raised. Many southern settlers preferred private institutions, subsidies by the state, and a highly decentralized district system. The affirmative vote was 78,523; the negative, 61,887.[72] In his third message Mills analyzed the vote to prove that the illiterate counties were the ones that voted "no" because, being illiterate, they did not understand the issue. In October 1854 his leadership in public education was recognized when he was elected Superintendent of Public Instruction, an office he held for about two and one-half years.

Other Indiana missionaries who deserve notice for their interest in public education include Moses H. Wilder, John Todd, P. S. Cleland, and Thomas Searle. Searle, Todd, James Welch, and W. W. Martin were Presbyterian ministers included in the committee of seven named to formulate the rather remarkable school system of 1824.[73]

Not all Presbyterians were so enthusiastic about the new

71. Ibid., pp. 408, 399, 402.   73. Boone, p. 23.
72. Boone, pp. 104–05. Monroe, *Founding of the American School System*, p. 291.

state schools. As the public school program gained momentum, a large body of the Old School Presbyterians became concerned. The church could not supervise the public schools, and she could not be happy with a divorce of religion and education. The Sunday School was not enough to substitute for religion integrated in the curriculum. In 1840 the Old School Assembly "accepted" a report calling for a system of church-controlled schools. In 1841 such a report was "adopted," but still without action to implement it. Pressures became still greater as educators and sectarian groups pressed for the secularization of public schools. Was all education now to be carried on by the state? Or were the church and state to set up divided but parallel systems? Or should all education be carried on by the church? By 1847 the Old School Presbyterians were engaged in a major experiment with parochial schools. Lewis J. Sherrill lists some 264 parochial schools that were founded by Presbyterians before the experiment was over.[74] The ranks of the Old School Presbyterians were never united in this enterprise. Charles Hodge of Princeton was for the parochial system, but Robert J. Breckinridge was State Superintendent of Education in Kentucky and a consistent opponent. Thomas Smyth of South Carolina favored the parochial schools, but J. H. Thornwell of that state opposed them. The New School Presbyterians had nothing to do with all this. When the Old School and the New School united in 1870, parochial schools were not discussed except for the comment that the new board of education was without instructions to maintain a school department.[75]

Indiana Synod, Old School, went strongly for parochial schools, founding twenty-five of them in the years 1847-70. Only Pennsylvania (43), New Jersey (36), and New York (28) had more than Indiana. The Presbyteries of Logansport,

74. *Presbyterian Parochial Schools, 1846–1870* (New Haven, Yale University, 1932), 261 pp.
75. Luther A. Weigle, from a paper prepared in memory of Lewis J. Sherrill and presented to the faculty of Union Seminary, New York, 1957, pp. 2–3.

Madison, and Salem committed themselves to the program.[76] When the members of Indianapolis Presbytery saw, in 1848, that a system of free schools with tax support was likely to be established by the next session of the Indiana legislature, they stated their belief that adequate religious instruction could not be given in such schools. Therefore they passed a resolution urging each congregation in the presbytery to establish a parochial school for the children of the members and such others as would attend. They declared it as their conviction that persons taxed to support free schools should be entitled to found their own schools and claim public education funds according to the number of children enrolled. This resolution and interpretation did not have unanimous support in the presbytery.[77] John Hendricks registered a formal protest against any petition for division of public funds to parochial schools, holding that the state government could not and should not grant it. The presbytery did not find Hendricks' reasons convincing, but in 1849 they heard the same conclusion from the synod: "With regard to petitioning the legislature of the State of Indiana for a division of the public school fund among the different denominations of Christians, or among schools established on the ground of elective affinity, and not by geographical boundaries Synod believe that such a petition would be inexpedient and injudicious."[78] Charles Hodge of Princeton thought that state funds should be divided to aid church schools, including the Roman Catholics. The majority of the Old School Presbyterians did not agree, however. Kingston church in Indiana was among the individual congregations to try for public funds for its parochial school. The attempt failed.

Presbyterians were also engaged in secondary education in Indiana. As a matter of fact, the use of the terms school,

76. Sherrill, pp. 35, 74–75. He draws both his story of a success (Hopewell) and his story of a failure (Indianapolis) from Indiana, pp. 160–68.
77. MIP, OS, *1*, 327–28, 330.   78. MIS, OS, *1*, 306–07.

seminary, academy, high school, college, and university was so loose in early Indiana that it is almost impossible to designate where secondary education began and ended. In the state system of schools there was to be the district school, the county seminary, and the state seminary or university representing a certain progression from elementary through secondary to collegiate education. In the Old School Presbyterian system the ideal of many was elementary education in the parochial school of the local church, secondary education in the academy of the presbytery, and collegiate training in the college of the synod. In practice however, neither the state nor the church provided all the levels. And the teachers most often began with the pupils at hand to give them whatever they needed. So loose, in fact, was the educational terminology that the Old School Presbyterians received an application from the "Primary Department" of "Highland University" of Highland, Kansas, asking aid as a parochial school![79]

Some of the private schools operated by Presbyterians offered training at the secondary level. Following 1819, Pastor W. W. Martin operated Martin's Academy at Livonia. Sometimes it is referred to as the "log college." Besides all the common branches, the school offered "higher mathematics, Greek, Latin, mental and moral philosophy, rhetoric, logic, and natural philosophy." The school thrived, bringing pupils from adjoining counties and even from outside the state. It was coeducational on the basis of principle. An impressive list of ministers, physicians, lawyers, and politicians were fitted for college by Martin, his wife, and his daughter.[80] John B. Anderson, son and brother of Presbyterian ministers, operated Anderson's High School for Boys at New Albany after 1840. Students came from all over the West to what the catalogue described as "a permanent English and classical school, in

79. Sherrill, p. 58; for lists of county seminaries and private seminaries see Boone, *Education in Indiana*, pp. 57–58, 60–61.
80. Boone, pp. 68–69. Alexander McPheeters, "A Brief History of the Livonia, Indiana, Presbyterian Churches, 1815–1874" (MS in Indiana Synod Office).

which young men might be prepared for the advanced classes in college, or for entering upon the business of life, professional or otherwise." Tuition and board, including fuel and lights, amounted to $31.25 per quarter of eleven weeks. French lessons were $5 extra, and vocal music under Professor Leonard $1 per quarter—washing per dozen, 38 cents.[81] Two of the secondary schools were destined to become colleges: the Finley Crowe Grammar School or Hanover Academy and the Wabash Manual Labor School and Teachers' Seminary at Crawfordsville. Private schools of this caliber set an educational standard that Indiana public schools had not begun to attain.

County seminaries were somewhat endowed by public lands and fees, but somewhat handicapped by being public property and therefore subject to factional strife in the frontier electorate:

> County people outside the town were then jealous of those within the corporation, and contended that schools supported by the county should not be located in the town. The old deserted seminary building at Vevay stands as a monument to this error. It was built under the Seminary Law. The first site was selected in Vevay but, after considerable delay caused by a protest by the country people, a site on a steep hill three hundred feet high, outside the corporation line, was chosen and the building erected. The country children could not get there but neither could the town children, so the country contingent was happy in the thought of equal rights.[82]

The seminary of Washington County at Salem came to be highly rated because it was conveniently located in the largest town in the county and because it had a very able teacher in

81. Emma Carleton, "An Early Indiana Educator," *IMH, I* (1905), 81–86.
82. Margaret S. Bird, "Early Education in Madison and Jefferson County, Indiana" (1944), p. 4. MS in possession of Mrs. R. W. Endicott.

the person of John I. Morrison. Occasionally a minister would teach such a school, as Boone indicates in his list of early teachers.[83]

Presbyterial academies were almost always superintended or taught by Presbyterian ministers. Thomas J. Hardin lists eight such academies: Delaney, at Newburgh (1842); Waveland (1849); Fort Wayne (ca. 1853); White Water, at Dunlapsville (1853); Blythe-Wood, at Petersburg (1853); Hopewell, near Franklin (1855); Barnett, at Charlestown (1860); and Lebanon Presbyterian, at Lebanon (1861).[84] In this list he does not consider the female academies at Greensburg, Hanover, Charlestown, and Logansport.

Eventually all these academies and seminaries either became colleges or, more probably, were displaced by the development of the public high school.[85] In their day they were the seed plot of higher education. Buley surmises that the pioneer academies and seminaries did for their day about what the colleges do now; they served about the same proportion of the population and about as well.[86] The evidence of Presbyterian leadership is overwhelming.[87] In these schools the Presbyterians perpetuated the classical education that they themselves had mastered, hardly raising the question whether it was what the frontiersman wanted or needed. Zion was to be built on such knowledge and virtue for all. Benjamin Cressy expressed this point of view in his address to Washington County Seminary at the height of its prosperity under Morrison:

> With all the enlarged views of a Pericles, Cicero, or the Antonines; it seems never to have entered their thoughts, that the common people had minds worthy of cultivation. Search the annals of the

83. *Education in Indiana*, pp. 52–55.
84. "The Academies of Indiana," *IMH, 10* (1914), 350–58.
85. John H. Fisher, "Primary and Secondary Education and the Presbyterian Church in the United States of America," *JPHS, 24* (1946), 13–43.
86. *Old Northwest, 2,* 342–43.
87. For examples of Presbyterian leadership in Indianapolis schools, see Julia Merrill, "Along Old Paths" (MS in Indiana State Library).

world, and not a solitary instance can be found, where the Christian religion has not prevailed, that the mass of mind in a nation has been so called into action as to constitute an enlightened community. Let science and religion, then, be encouraged; and ignorance and vice, with all their concomitants of woe, shall recede before the blazing light of that day, when *incense and pure offering shall arise from every heart;*—when nation after nation shall catch the loud chorus,—*peace on earth, good will to men,*—and the world, itself, shall be raised to that elevation, to which the human powers seem destined by the great Proprietor of the universe.[88]

Presbyterians were especially active in the leadership of Indiana's early colleges. In Merrill E. Gaddis' view the Protestant sects succeeded on the frontier in inverse ratio to their intellectual attainments and in direct ratio to their emotional appeal.[89] Both the Presbyterians and the colleges were exotic on Indiana's frontier. They represented a projection of eastern scholastic standards which the Hoosier settler found hard to tolerate. However, for the training of ministers, for raising up all the learned professions, and for the general building up of Zion, the Presbyterians had to have colleges. Fourteen of the forty colleges and universities that were established in the United States between 1780 and 1829 were located west of the Alleghenies. Seven of the fourteen were founded by Presbyterians, one by Presbyterians and Congregationalists together, one by Episcopalians, one by Baptists, and the remaining four by the states. All these state institutions were started under Presbyterian influence.[90]

Samuel Scott was the first resident Presbyterian preacher in Indiana. From 1810 to 1823 he was also organizer, principal,

88. *An Address Delivered before the Zelo-Paideusian Society of Washington County Seminary, 14 March 1834* (Salem, 1834), p. 17.
89. "Religious Ideas and Attitudes in the Early Frontier," *CH,* 2 (1933), 158.
90. Sweet, *Presbyterians, Vol. 2 of Religion on the American Frontier,* pp. 75–76.

and teacher of Vincennes University—a territorial university backed by a Congressional grant of a township of land in 1804. Twenty-three trustees administered the grant; they sold enough land to build a brick building for $6,000 and engage Scott as principal. The aim of the legislature was large. Vincennes was to offer the classical liberal arts program. As soon as feasible, there were to be graduate schools for each of the "three learned professions." In addition, the legislators provided for the education of girls and Indians—a large and liberal charter indeed. No particular system of religion was to be taught and the school was to be available to patrons of any creed or no creed. For years it was the collegiate institution farthest west. But from the beginning it was in financial difficulty. The legislature authorized a $20,000 lottery to procure "the necessary philosophical and experimental apparatus", but the lottery was not held. Fees of students were almost the sole support. Soon after the retirement of Scott, the university closed for lack of funds and the land grant passed to the state seminary at Bloomington. [91]

The act of Congress of 1816 which enabled Indiana to organize as a state also provided for the founding of a state seminary. An additional township of land was granted; after four years it could be sold to benefit the state school. Such a state university was included in the constitutional provision for a school system. President Madison designated a township in Monroe County as the land grant. A youthful Presbyterian elder named David H. Maxwell had been a delegate to the conventions to form a state government and frame the constitution. In 1819 Maxwell moved to Bloomington in Monroe County and that year the First Presbyterian Church of Bloomington was organized in Maxwell's cabin by Isaac Reed. Elder Maxwell kept his eye on that land-grant township, and as soon as the four years had expired he lobbied forcefully to locate the state school in Bloomington. The deed was done in

91. Boone, *Education in Indiana*, pp. 15–19. James A. Woodburn, *Higher Education in Indiana* (Washington, D.C., 1891), pp. 30–35.

1820, and Maxwell was named to the board of trustees — he was president of the board until his death in 1854.[92]

It was probably through the influence of David Maxwell and Isaac Reed that Reed's brother-in-law, Baynard Hall, was invited to the West. When the new state seminary buildings were partly constructed, he was chosen to open the school and serve as its principal. Hall was a Presbyterian minister born in Philadelphia and trained in theology at Princeton. School opened in the spring of 1824. In spite of the advertisements about a classical and mathematical school, a nondescript host of boys reported for classes believing that "by some magic art, our hero *could*, and being paid by government, *should*, and without putting anybody to the expense of books and implements, touch and transmute all and in less than no time, into great scholars." Hall weeded out the ten who were ready to begin with Latin, Greek, and algebra and sent the rest home over protest. "Daddy says he doesn't see no sort a use in the high larn'd things—and he wants me to larn Inglish only, and bookkeepin, and surveyin, so as to tend store and run a line." "I allow, Mister, we've near on about as good a right to be larn'd what we want, as them tother fellers on that bench;—it's a free school for all."[93] This or any selectivity was resented and attributed to the Presbyterian professor. The resentment grew to fury when the people, who argued that the professor ought to serve for the honor, were asked to pay $10 a year tuition. They considered Hall "the feller what tuk hire for teaching and preaching, and was gettin to be a big-bug on the poor people's edicashin money."[94] When the word got out that the board of trustees was about to elect a second professor and that he, too, was a Presbyterian, the cries "sectarianism" and "aristocrat" were loud in Bloomington. A noisy local delegation burst into the trustee's meeting to protest another Presbyterian professor,

92. Louise Maxwell, "Sketch of Dr. David H. Maxwell," *IMH, 8* (1912), 101–08. "Maxwell, David Hervey," *Dictionary of American Biography, 12.*
93. *New Purchase*, pp. 322, 324.
94. Ibid., p. 321.

but John Harney of Kentucky was elected anyway.[95] The first four professors of the state school were Presbyterian; of the numerical dominance of Presbyterians there can be no question. To the hypersensitive frontiersmen this spelled aristocracy and the union of church and state. Such charges have been made and copied by historians.

The fairly standard format for stating the charges is that state funds for educational purposes in Indiana, as elsewhere in the West, were for many years under the control of Presbyterians. These Presbyterians viewed themselves as especial guardians and patrons of education, indeed the only competent educators of the people. Other religious groups, notably the Methodists, protested this Presbyterian monopoly but were cavalierly treated. On these grounds the Methodists established DePauw University as a school of their own.[96]

Any objective account of the controversy ought to consider three documents. The first is the account by Baynard Hall, whose testimony is biased in favor of the Presbyterians but who was a key participant writing a first-hand description.[97] The second is the statement of the fifteen trustees of the state school made 8 December 1830. They flatly deny any sectarianism and conclude: "Of this board it is believed four are Presbyterians, or at least were so educated; four Protestant Episcopalians; three Baptists; two Methodists; one Covenanter; and one a member of the Christian Society or Church. Out of such a mixture of religious opinion it cannot reasonably be supposed, that a majority could be prevailed upon to establish, or in any respect to countenance a sectarian domination."[98] The third has to do with the political capital to be made of these charges. It is the letter of Indianapolis attorney Alexander Davidson to his brother in Lexington, Virginia:

95. James A. Woodburn, *History of Indiana University* (2 vols. Bloomington, University, 1940), *1*, 16–21. Hall, pp. 327–34.

96. F. C. Holliday, *Indiana Methodism* (Cincinnati, 1873), pp. 317–20. See also Sweet, *Circuit-Rider Days*, pp. 60–62.

97. *New Purchase*, pp. 319–34, 563–66, and passim.

98. Woodburn, *Indiana University*, *1*, 76.

We are just on the eve of our election, and, if you ever look into the Spirit of '40, which I send to grandpa, you will see that it is hotly contested. Until within a few days we were electing our candidate for Governor, but matters have assumed a new phase. The attempt has been made, & I fear with some success to array the whole Methodist Church against Gov. Bigger, and for these very grave reasons:—Some 12 years ago the Methodist Conference memorialized the legislature to appoint a Methodist minister Professor in the Indiana University. Two ministers who were written to on the subject replied that there was no one in the Conference whom they could safely recommend for the station. Upon the faith of that statement, Bigger (who was then a member of the legislature) moved to lay the memorial on the table with the simple remark that there was no minister in the State of that denomination qualified to fill the place of professor. This charge has slept until Whitcomb the loco candidate for gov. waked it up & has bruited it all over the state with all the improvements & additions that an artful demagogue was capable of making to it. The other reason (& with them the most weighty) is that the notice given for the meeting of the Education Convention which was held in Indianapolis last winter (& over which Gov. Bigger happened to preside) the President of the Methodist College in Indiana was called *professor* & this is esteemed a blow at the *dignity* of their church! Oh, most weighty reasons! Oh, ineffable asses! If our candidate is defeated it will be from this cause . . . the Methodist vote in this State is large.[99]

Serious charges of sectarianism were hurled in the political arena of the state legislature. Was the sectarianism there? The faculty, the students, the board of trustees, the legislative com-

99. 28 July 1843. This letter is torn but readable.

mittees—all said it was not. But these firm denials were of little use against the malcontents' warnings that there was bound to be sectarianism when all three members of the faculty were Presbyterians. Some extreme democrats even proposed amending the college charter so that no two professors or teachers might be of the same religious sect! This would certainly have been an unconstitutional religious test for public office.[100]

Hanover College was born of Indiana's need for ministers. Those who came from the East were not enough; they were likely to return to the East or to be stricken by illness. The only hope for a supply of ministers was to raise them on the ground. The Presbytery of Salem took action at its first meeting, in 1824, by naming an education committee to find a way to prepare poor but pious young men for the ministry. John Finley Crowe was chairman.[101] By 1825 a plan was advanced for a Presbyterian academy at Hanover to be operated on the manual labor system. When the committee could not secure another competent teacher, it asked Crowe to organize and teach the school.[102] In 1827 he opened a grammar school at his house with six boys "not one of whom was pious, though all sons of the church." The next year there was a revival at the town of Hanover. Forty-six professed their faith, including eight of the fourteen students at the academy. Enrollment increased considerably. In 1828 the school was chartered by the state and in 1829 adopted by Indiana Synod as a synodical school. Also in 1829 a theological department was added for graduate training for the ministry.

Hanover passed through all the perils of storm, poverty, and division. In June 1837 a tornado demolished one wing of the college building and the house of Professor Niles. Some college books and papers were actually blown across the river

---

100. Woodburn, *1*, 75–76.   101. MSP, *1*, 8.

102. For a reprint of a "Succinct History of Hanover College" by John Finley Crowe, see William A. Millis, *The History of Hanover College from 1827 to 1927* (Hanover, the College, 1927), pp. 11–18.

into Kentucky.[103] The faculty was always limited. Even with
the enlarged staff of 1832, James Blythe was appointed "President, and Professor of Moral Science, Chemistry, and
Natural Philosophy." John Finley Crowe was "Vice President,
and Professor of Logic, Rhetoric, Belles Lettres, etc." M. A. H.
Niles was "Professor of the Greek, Latin, and French Languages" and John H. Harney "Professor of Mathematics and
Astronomy." When Erasmus D. MacMaster came to be president, he felt things were so bad at Hanover that the best procedure was to move to Madison and offer the synod a charter
of a completely new institution. MacMaster convinced a
majority of the board of trustees, sixty students, and all of the
faculty but John Finley Crowe. This professor stayed on to
operate Old Hanover; he won back the students, was re-
approved by both the synod and the state, and helped a new
president raise an endowment of $40,000.[104] The college
weathered every test. At the end of twenty-five years 223 students had graduated; 126 were ministers; 36 were teachers; 130
others had entered the ministry without graduating. James H.
Johnston commented in 1865 that of 124 Old School ministers
in Indiana, 44 had been students of Hanover College.[105]

Wabash was Indiana's only college of the Presbyterian-
Congregational or New School type. The southern population discouraged the Yankee college builders.[106] Five missionaries of the American Home Missionary Society, however, had
chosen the Upper Wabash Valley as their field of labor. There
was no literary institution north of Bloomington, and the need
for ministers was critical. There were around fifteen young men

103. In a letter from Amos W. Butler, Indianapolis, to Glenn Culbertson,
    Hanover, 29 Jan. 1920 (MS in Indiana State Library).
104. Woodburn, *Higher Education*, pp. 169–70. Erasmus D. MacMaster,
    Speech in the Synod of Indiana, 4 October 1844 in Relation to Madison University
    (Madison, 1844).
105. *Ministry of Forty Years*, p. 23.
106. Donald G. Tewksbury, *The Founding of American Colleges and Universities
    Before the Civil War with Particular Reference to the Religious Influence upon
    the College Movement* (New York, Columbia University, 1932).

183

in the Wabash country who would study for the ministry if they could have facilities. So it was that Williamson Dunn of Crawfordsville donated fifteen acres, the citizens of Crawfordsville made a liberal subscription, and Caleb Mills of Andover Seminary was engaged to open the school in December 1833. Progress to 1838 was remarkable. The state issued a charter to Wabash Manual Labor College and Teachers' Seminary in 1834; students and staff increased; Elihu W. Baldwin came from his pastorate in New York to be president. In the fall of 1838 a large college building was completed and a library collected. But that winter the new building was destroyed by fire: " One of the most painful sights during the night of that fearful conflagration, was the sight of the half consumed leaves of our beautiful and valuable library bourne up amid the whirling columns of smoke and flames of that dismal scene. It was a choice collection of about two thousand volumes, exclusive of the text book library. Brick and mortar and timber have been replaced, but we are still compelled to feel most keenly the loss of our books."[107] These were depression times. The school had to carry on with little operating capital and a debt of $8,000 because of the fire. In 1840 the much-beloved President Baldwin died. The debt was finally liquidated in 1846 and the endowment increased. Fund raising in the East was often a touchy business because the western settlers did not care to have funds raised for their conversion or improvement. Politicians made the most of any popular distaste. Wabash College President Charles White was on an eastern tour when Professor E. O. Hovey wrote him in 1848:

> I suppose ere this you have heard of excitement awakened by an anonymous report of your speech made in New Haven, published in the Christian Advocate and Journal. The poor West has been greatly abased! We say but little about it, waiting for you to tell the people what you said and why you said

107. Caleb Mills, *Sermon, Preached at Crawfordsville on the Sabbath before the Commencement in Wabash College, 18 July 1841* (Indianapolis, 1841), p. 9.

it. A number of our Methodist friends felt much hurt that they should have been bro't into the same category with Mormons and Millerites. And some Democratic papers made a heavy blow upon the whole matter. But I trust no serious harm will result.

A pretty strong current of prejudice has been awakened by the remarks of J. in the Advocate, and the diabolical comments thereon by political papers in the state. J. is a James Foley of New Haven and has written to this effect, that if you deny what he has said he will publish *more* and *worse*. A newspaper controversy is what we have always aimed to avoid.[108]

Hovey tried to avoid popular clamor but he would not conciliate it. There was some speculation that Charles White had too much refinement to succeed as president of a western college. Hovey recorded his dissent: "We think a President, and the other officers of College, should bring their pupils *up* to a good degree of refinement of taste and manners, rather than be perfectly *hoosierized themselves.* The fact is great efforts must be made to educate and elevate minds in the west, or it will exist only, we fear, to wield a tremendous, it may be fatal . . . force against the best institutions of the land. Somebody must do it—it will cost sacrifice—yet it will be attended with much pleasure—its result must be happy in high degree."[109]

Indiana Theological Seminary is Indiana's early venture into postgraduate education. It began as a department of theology in Hanover College in 1829; its history is a sorry story of nonsupport. The plan was that the Synod of Indiana would name the professors, raise the money, and supervise the operation of this graduate school of theology as a department of Hanover College. In that way the theological school could benefit from the facilities and the faculty of the college, and perhaps it could contribute something to campus life as well.

108. Crawfordsville, 10 Dec. 1848, 16 Dec. 1848 (MSS in Indiana State Library).
109. Ibid., 5 May 1841.

The synod made elaborate plans, appointed directors, examined the students and faculty, made pleas to the presbyteries and churches, but raised no money. The seminary was never solvent. For example, in 1833 the seminary directors reported that there were five theological students who had been duly examined. However, the synod had paid only about one-third of the professor's salary (there was only one professor); and even with the efforts of the college to help, they were now $587 in arrears on an annual salary of $600. Further, a second professor was named at that meeting of the synod, and there appeared no prospect of paying his salary. Hanover College wanted to be reimbursed for the money it had advanced to the theological professors. In 1834 an arrangement was made whereby the trustees of Hanover would take over the seminary and ask the Synods of Illinois, Indiana, Kentucky, Cincinnati, and Ohio to join in support. By 1836 Hanover College recommended that the seminary secure a separate and distinct charter from the state and sever its connection with Hanover College. The next year the seminary claimed ten students, three graduates, and twelve alumni, but it also admitted that only three churches in the synod had supported the school, and that the board was indebted $1,000 to one professor. Matters improved a little after the Old School–New School division. The seminary belonged to the Old School and could hope to be supported in that loyalty. The synod became more systematic; instead of issuing a general statement of urgency they issued quotas to the presbyteries and raised half the amount requested, almost certainly a new high in support. [110]

When Mr. Ayers of New Albany promised to make gifts totaling $15,000 if the seminary would move to New Albany, it appeared to be the hand of Providence. The move was made in 1841. But even darker days were ahead. Indiana Theological Seminary tried to stay neutral on slavery when the students of her seven synods were choosing sides. Those who were antislavery went to Lane Seminary; those in sympathy with the

110. MIS, *1*, 72–85, 163–66, 183–85, 221, 243. MIS, OS, *1*, 47, 68, 70.

South went to the Old School seminary at Danville after 1853. Few came to New Albany. Indiana Theological Seminary closed its doors after commencement in 1857. Thus the transfer to Chicago in 1859 was only nominal. The relocation came when Cyrus Hall McCormick, a stout conservative of the Old School, offered to endow four professors at $25,000 each if the General Assembly would take control from the synods and locate the seminary in Chicago. The Assembly took the action, but control was really in the hands of McCormick, who kept a watchful eye out to assure a rigid Old School doctrine and a policy of silence on slavery. His control was exercised through his gifts. The seminary opened in a Chicago hotel in 1859 and very nearly failed again. But as the Civil War progressed, Danville was in the theater of operations, and so Danville lost while Chicago gained. Cyrus McCormick's views were not determinative, and some remnant of Indiana Theological Seminary went on to notable service in the church.[111]

The plain conclusion is that Indiana Presbyterians viewed higher education as the very capstone of Hoosier Zion. Religion and learning were to enlighten and move the world:

> We know that it is our aim to bring over and into the institution the influence of the principles of the gospel of the Son of God. It is our design to mingle the waters of the Pierian spring with those of the well of Bethlehem, and of "Siloa's fount, that flows fast by the Oracle of God!" It is our wish to graft the laurel of Parnassus into the vine that is planted upon the top of Zion's mount. It is our desire that the Minerva of our college may be baptized into Christ, and be inspired by the Spirit of the Highest.
>
> May we not hope that thus under this union of religion and learning, here on the banks of our beautiful Ohio, amid hills, and ravines, rocks, and cascades,

111. William T. Hutchinson, *Cyrus Hall McCormick* (2 vols. New York, Appleton-Century, 1935), 2, 3–36.

and forests, our institution will grow up, and strengthen, and enlarge; and co-operating with other similar institutions, will aid in pouring the life-giving light of science and Christianity over this great land from the tops of the Alleghenies to those of the Rocky Mountains and from the great seas of the north to the Andes of the south, and far hence to the nations that sit in darkness and in the region and shadow of death.[112]

112. Erasmus D. MacMaster, *A Discourse on the Occasion of the Author's Inauguration as President of Hanover College* (Hanover, 1838), p. 36.

CONCLUSION

The State of Indiana had changed by 1850. Her population had reached 988,416 according to census records. A public school system seemed assured and every Indiana youth might expect to receive a modicum of education. Along with the whole of the Old Northwest, the state had formed commercial ties with the East instead of the South; facile transportation had made this possible. In a few years the Civil War was to create the impression that southern influence north of the Ohio had been swept away. To some it must have appeared that the Ohio Valley was truly a suburb of Boston and a great new day had come.

Richard Power has pointed out that this Yankee victory was apparent but far from complete in the Old Northwest: "It has already been noted that the Yankees after about 1850 regarded themselves as victors in a 'thirty years war.' There was much to make this view plausible. It was easy during those years to be swept into overstatement by the delirious intemperance of Manifest Destiny. But the New England triumph, however large, was never so complete as the zealots believed."[1] This was especially true of Indiana, where south-

1. *Corn Belt Culture*, p. 170.

ern back-country culture was so predominant. Settlers from the northeastern states and immigrants from Europe settled beside the southern stock. There was intermingling but at a stage far short of Yankee victory or even homogenization. Indiana remained Hoosier in her language, in her moods of isolation, in her resentment of outsiders, and in her toleration of local demagogues.

Indiana is different now than she was in her early days, but she is also much the same. The immigration corridors of Indiana have remained open from south to north. A common saying in mid-twentieth century is that Kentucky has taken Indianapolis without firing a shot. In these days of high mobility, Indiana shares this population stream from the Appalachian South with her sister states of the Old Northwest and with the urban centers of the whole nation. As in the early days, there is a minority of genteel and educated southerners who are welcomed everywhere. But there are hosts of so-called "southern whites" who are poorly trained technically and socially. These latter are the modern upland southerners seeking their place in the sun. That place is less in the squatter's cabin in the woods now than in the wilderness of the industrial cities. But the hovels are the same. The drive to make a new economic start and the resentment of the "educated big bug" are still there. Extensive Southern Appalachian studies have just been made with the aid of a grant from the Ford Foundation. The results are even more vivid than some had guessed: high birth rate, low income, poor education, small economic opportunity, high mobility. Indiana has changed, but in view of this migration her population problems will be much like those of the century and a half since 1800.

The church in Indiana changed too. The Christian faith did keep pace with the early settlers in a way. All the churches grew, but they did not grow equally by any means. The Roman Catholics, the Episcopalians, the Lutherans, and the Moravians grew slowly, more by immigration and by increase from natural birth rate than by evangelization of the unchurched settlers. In 1850 Indiana had eighty-nine congregations of Friends, ranking fourth in the nation in the number of Friends' churches that year. But it was evangelical Protestantism which carried the day, especially the denominations which were identified with the folkways of the upland South. In 1850 the Methodists in Indiana had 779 churches with accommodations for 266,372 worshipers; their church property in the state was valued at $492,560. The Baptists reported 403 churches, with accommodations for 138,783 and property valued at $212,735. The Christian Church, now but an infant among the denominations, had 187 churches in Indiana, some of them honored as the first churches to be established in the pioneer communities.

The Presbyterians also grew. By 1850 they had 282 churches in Indiana, with accommodations for 105,582 worshipers (about ten times the official membership of the Old School and New School combined) and church property valued at $326,520. Since the earliest frontier days, there had been little change in the requirements for the ministry, except that graduation from college and theological seminary became quite generally expected. The Presbyterians had set themselves to their mission in the West with a small body of trained clergy. That decision meant that they had to be sharply limited in the breadth of their ministry; in the case of Indiana it meant that the Presbyterians could not really occupy the state in the crucial early years.

Since 1850 the major denominations have grown more and more alike. Presbyterians have learned more flexibility and have learned to carry their ministry to the people more winsomely. The popular frontier churches—Methodist, Baptist, Christian—have moved admirably to raise their standards. The itinerant minister, the uneducated farmer-preacher, and the "see-saw-hum-and-spit" manner are nearly gone. The pattern in each denomination is an educated ministry with a deliberate plan of community ministry. However pleasing these changes may be, they must be recognized as expensive. Many Hoosiers who felt at home with the older folk churches have failed to make the transition to the new. There is a painful gap between them and their educated clergy; they keep murmuring about the old-time religion. Some have withdrawn to sect groups with the old, comfortable, rural, southern ways.

As for the new southern white who is now migrating to the North, he finds little to attract him to the major denominations. Studies show that in his southern home he is the least church connected and the poorest church attender of all Americans. If he is church connected at all, it is likely to be with a sect group which relates him very little to a well-rounded community life. When he moves north, he attends his church even less than he did back home.

Early Presbyterians in Indiana did not fail when they refused to identify with back-country culture. They were a healthy corrective on the frontier because they presented another cultural and religious standard which the frontiersmen needed to remember and to face. Nor did the early folk religions in Indiana fail because they were so close to the woods dwellers. At least they kept a vital form of Christianity alive as an option for thousands who might never otherwise have met the faith. The peculiar mission of the churches of Indiana today is much less clear. All the major Protestant denominations have become alike and minister to the same population strata—strata in which the new southern settlers are not included. But the persistent back-country mentality and the continuing immigration from the South are a problem to all these churches. The perennial Hoosiers, even the urbanized ones, are no easier to win than their forebears were.

BIBLIOGRAPHY

Despite the loss by fire in 1937 of a valuable collection of papers, there is no dearth of materials on the early Presbyterians in Indiana. The researcher faces an almost overwhelming wealth of original materials, few of them catalogued or evaluated. The best depositories are at Indianapolis: the storage vault in the Indiana Synod building and the Indiana Department of the Indiana State Library. The Presbyterian Historical Society at Philadelphia duplicates many of these items in its collection.

The records or minutes of the Indiana Synod are available from the founding of the synod in 1826 to the present. At the synod meeting in 1926 the stated clerk was commissioned to transcribe the old handwritten records. In 1943 stated clerk S. Arthur Stewart reported that the following minute books had been transcribed and the original handwritten volumes deposited with the Presbyterian Historical Society in Philadelphia:

> 1826–1845 Synod of Indiana (N.S.)
> 1846–1850 Synod of Indiana (N.S.)
> 1859–1869 Synod of Indiana (N.S.)
> 1839–1848 Synod of Indiana (O.S.)
> 1849–1861 Synod of Indiana (O.S.)

1861–1870 Synod of Indiana (O.S.)
1870–1875 Synod of Southern Indiana
1875–1882 Synod of Southern Indiana
1851–1869 Synod of the Wabash
1843–1865 Synod of Northern Indiana
1865–1868 Synod of Northern Indiana
1869–1879 Synod of Northern Indiana
1870–1882 Synod of Indiana
1882–1885 Synod of Indiana

The clerk's careful typescript has been placed in every major depository of Presbyterian historical papers. Citations of synod minutes in this paper use the paging of the typescript.

The records or minutes of most Indiana presbyteries are collected at the synod vault at Indianapolis. Of particular value are the minutes of Salem Presbytery, pioneer presbytery of Indiana and regions to the west, beginning in 1824. Presbytery minutes through 1850 at the synod vault include Salem; Salem (O.S.); Salem (N.S.); Indianapolis; Indianapolis (O.S.); Indianapolis (N.S.); Madison; Vincennes; Greencastle; Muncie; LaPorte; Lake; and Whitewater. Every continuing presbytery has prepared some sort of history. Some have done two or more revisions. Perhaps the most persistent history writer is Indianapolis Presbytery, while the best single effort is Fort Wayne Presbytery's *Forest, Fort, and Faith* prepared by George William Allison.

Records or minutes of local church sessions are filed at the synod storage vault. But they are also in storage in Philadelphia, in local banks, in local churches, in pastors' studies, and in private homes. To pursue a plan for writing the synod's history is to invite a deluge of these, each with a fascinating local story to unfold. The same is true of histories and centennial booklets of local churches. Research in this project has included poring over scores of them ranging from a superb documentary collection like the 400-page *Centennial Memorial of the First Presbyterian Church of Indianapolis*, or the equally long *First Presbyterian Church of Franklin, One Hundred and Twenty Years*, to an unidentified reprint of a few local newspaper clippings. No study is valid which cannot meet the test of these specific histories. However, the direct use of particular church records must be limited in the interest of broader interpretation.

Among the American Home Missionary Society Papers are the detailed quarterly reports of missionaries in the West to the executive secretary of the Society in New York. These reports are usually in letter form. Chicago Theological Seminary is the depository for the papers; Indiana State Library has obtained photostat (1825–35) or microfilm (1836–93) copies of the reports pertaining to Indiana. There are literally hundreds of letters from early Indiana missionaries, constituting an unequaled source of firsthand historical data.

Indiana ministers read many church periodicals produced outside the state and often subscribed for their parishioners. They were influenced by these periodicals and contributed to them. Reports from Indiana appeared in the *Presbyterian*, the *Home Missionary*, and many others. Synods and presbyteries sent off extracts from their proceedings to be published in the *Western Presbyterian Herald* or the *Watchman of the Valley*. Local papers gave generous space to the doings of the Presbyterians. The *Indiana Religious Intelligencer* was the most ambitious early publication effort of the synod; it was issued from 1828 to 1830 as a weekly clipsheet with bits of local news. Broken files of the *Intelligencer* are available in the Indiana State Library and at the Presbyterian Historical Society.

There are occasional items on Indiana Presbyterians in the Shane Papers at the Presbyterian Historical Society, the Fletcher Papers and the Maxwell Papers at Indiana State Library, and the Wilson Papers at the University of Kentucky. Most interesting of all is the collection of Hovey Letters at Indiana State Library; Mr. and Mrs. E. O. Hovey sent them from Fountain County and from Wabash College in the period from 1826 to 1859.

Some historical writings of early Presbyterian ministers themselves are of particular value. Isaac Reed kept a journal of much of his work in Indiana. He published that journal, along with certain personal papers and church papers, as *The Christian Traveller*. In 1828 John M. Dickey published his *Brief History of the Presbyterian Church in the State of Indiana*, thus recording his firsthand knowledge of all the early churches and ministers in the state. Two manuscript volumes entitled *History of the Presbyterian Church in Indiana* are not marked as to author or compiler, but there appears indisputable internal and external evidence that Dickey is the writer. Baynard Hall's autobiographical volume *The New Purchase* is both valuable and delightful. James H. Johnston, in his *Ministry of Forty Years in Indiana*, expertly summarized the progress of Presbyterianism in the state as he had participated in it to 1865. In that same year P. S. Cleland of Greenwood published his *Quarter-Century Discourse* after twenty-five years as pastor of the local church. M. M. Post recorded his efforts in Northern Indiana in *A Retrospect after Thirty Years' Ministry at Logansport.*

Among the more general sources, the minutes of the General Assemblies and kindred official publications of both Old School and New School should be noted. R. C. Buley's interpretation of *The Old Northwest, 1815–1840* and the stimulating studies of Richard L. Power are an excellent general setting for this Presbyterian story. There is a wealth of travel accounts of early Indiana, the best being collected in Harlow Lindley's *Indiana as Seen by Early Travelers.* Hanford Edson's *Contributions to the Early History of the Presbyterian Church in Indiana* (1898) is a valuable collection of materials which invite interpretation.

Allison, G. W., *Forest, Fort, and Faith: Historical Sketches of the Presbytery of Fort Wayne, Organized January 2, 1845,* 1945.

Armstrong, M. W., L. A. Loetscher, C. Anderson, eds., *The Presbyterian Enterprise, Sources of American Presbyterian History,* Philadelphia, Westminster, 1956.

Barnard, J. H., "Sketch of Early Presbyterianism in Indiana," *IMH,* 21 (1925), 300–10.

Bishop, R. H., *An Outline of the History of the Church in the State of Kentucky, during a period of Forty Years,* Lexington, Kentucky, Skillman, 1824.

Boone, R. C., *A History of Education in Indiana,* New York, Appleton, 1892.

Brown, J. H., "Presbyterian Beginnings in Ohio," dissertation. University of Pittsburgh, 1952.

Buley, R. C., *The Old Northwest Pioneer Period 1815–1840*, 2 vols. Indianapolis, Indiana Historical Society, 1950.

Cady, J. F., *The Origin and Development of the Missionary Baptist Church in Indiana*, Franklin, Indiana, Franklin College 1942.

Cauble, W., *Disciples of Christ in Indiana: Achievements of a Century*, Indianapolis, Meigs, 1930.

Centennial Memorial: First Presbyterian Church, Indianapolis, Indiana, Indianapolis, the Church, 1925.

Clark, M. B., "The Old Log College at Livonia," *IMH*, 23 (1927), 73–81.

Cleland, P. S., *A Quarter-Century Discourse, Delivered at Greenwood, Indiana, 18 December 1864 at the Twenty-fifth Anniversary of His Ministry to the Presbyterian Church in That Place*, Indianapolis, Holloway, Douglas, 1865.

Davidson, R., *History of the Presbyterian Church in the State of Kentucky*, New York, Carter, 1847.

DesChamps, M. B., "The Presbyterian Church in the South Atlantic States 1801–1861," dissertation, Emory University, 1952.

Dickey, J. M., *A Brief History of the Presbyterian Church in the State of Indiana*, Madison, Indiana, Arion, 1828.

———"Early History of the Presbyterian Church in Indiana Giving Biographies of Ministers and Annals of the Churches," 2 vols. 1848, MS in Indiana State Library.

Drury, C. M., *Presbyterian Panorama: One Hundred Fifty Years of National Missions History*, Philadelphia, Presbyterian Board of Christian Education, 1952.

Edson, H. A., *Contributions to the Early History of the Presbyterian Church in Indiana*, Cincinnati, Winona, 1898.

Esarey, L., *A History of Indiana from Its Exploration to 1850*, 2 vols. Fort Wayne, Indiana, Hoosier Press, 1924.

Fisher, J. H., "Primary and Secondary Education and the Presbyterian Church in the United States of America," *JPHS*, 24 (1946), 13–43.

Geiger, C. H., *The Program of Higher Education of the Presbyterian Church USA*, Cedar Rapids, Laurance, 1940.

Gillett, E. H., *History of the Presbyterian Church in the United States of America*, 2 vols. Philadelphia, Presbyterian Publication Committee, 1864.

Goodykoontz, C. B., *Home Missions on the American Frontier*, Caldwell, Idaho, Caston, 1939.

Hall, B. R., *The New Purchase: or, Seven and a Half Years in the Far West*, by Robert Carlton, esq. (pseud.), ed. James A. Woodburn, Indiana Centennial Edition, Princeton University Press, 1916.

Heller, H. L., *The Indiana Conference of the Methodist Church 1832–1956*, Historical Society of Indiana Conference, 1956.

Hovey, E. O., "History of Wabash College," *Wabash Magazine*, 1 (1857), 193–239.

Johnson, C. A., *The Frontier Camp Meeting; Religion's Harvest Time*, Dallas, Southern Methodist University Press, 1955.

Johnston, J. H., *A Ministry of Forty Years in Indiana*, Indianapolis, Holloway, Douglas, 1865.

Kuhns, F., "The Operations of the American Home Missionary Society in the Old Northwest, 1826–1851," dissertation, University of Chicago, 1947.

Lindley, H., ed., *Indiana as Seen by Early Travelers: A Collection of Reprints from Books of Travel, Letters and Diaries prior to 1830*, Indianapolis, Indiana Historical Commission, 1916.

McAvoy, T. T., *The Catholic Church in Indiana, 1789–1834*, New York, Columbia University Press, 1940.

McKinney, W. W., ed., *The Presbyterian Valley*, Pittsburgh, Davis and Warde, 1958.

Millis, W. A., *History of Hanover College from 1827 to 1927*, Hanover, Indiana, the College, 1927.

Moores, C. W., *Caleb Mills and the Indiana School System*, IHSP, 3 (Indianapolis, 1905), 359–638.

Osborne, J. I., and T. G. Gronert, *Wabash College; The First Hundred Years, 1832–1932*, Crawfordsville, Indiana, Banta, 1932.

Palmer, H. C., *The First Presbyterian Church of Franklin, Indiana: One Hundred and Twenty Years, 1824–1944*, Franklin, the Church, 1946.

Posey, W. B., *The Presbyterian Church in the Old Southwest, 1778–1838*, Richmond, John Knox, 1952.

Post, M. M., *A Retrospect after Thirty Years' Ministry at Logansport, Indiana*, Logansport, Brighhurst, 1860.

Power, R. L., *Planting Corn Belt Culture: The Impress of the Upland Southerner and Yankee in the Old Northwest*, IHSP, 17 (Indianapolis, 1953), 196 pp.

Presbyterianism in Indiana, Centennial Meeting of the Synod in Vincennes, 1926, Gary, Calumet Press, 1926.

Reed, I., *The Christian Traveller*, New York, Harper, 1828.

Rule, L. V., *The Light Bearers*, Louisville, Brandt, 1926.

Rule, L. V., "Pen Portraits of Presbyterian Pioneers," MS in Presbyterian Historical Society Library, Philadelphia.

————"Samuel Shannon, Giant of God in Old Salem Presbytery," MS in Indiana State Library.

Sherrill, L. J., *Presbyterian Parochial Schools, 1846–1870*, New Haven, Yale University Press, 1932.

Slosser, G. J., ed., *They Seek a Country: The American Presbyterians*, New York, Macmillan, 1955.

Sweet, W. W., *Circuit-Rider Days in Indiana*, Indianapolis, Stewart, 1916.

————"Early Methodist Circuits in Indiana," *IMH, 10* (1914), 359–68.

————*The Presbyterians*, Vol. 2 of *Religion on the American Frontier, 1783–1840*, 4 vols. Chicago University Press, 1936.

Thomas, J. H., "The Academies of Indiana," *IMH, 10* (1914), 331–58.

Thompson, R. E., *A History of the Presbyterian Churches in the United States*, New York, Christian Literature, 1895.

Trinterud, L. J., *The Forming of an American Tradition: A Reexamination of Colonial Presbyterianism*, Philadelphia, Westminster, 1949.

Vander Velde, L. G., *The Presbyterian Churches and the Federal Union, 1861–1869*, Cambridge, Harvard University Press, 1932.

Wishard, E. M., *William Henry Wishard, A Doctor of the Old School*, Indianapolis, Hollenbeck, 1920.

Woodburn, J. A., *History of Indiana University*, 2 vols. Bloomington, the University, 1940.

INDEX

✠ INDEX ✠

reports, 20, 22–24, 29, 52–57, 66, 76, 81, 86, 90, 98, 123, 137, 145–46, 154–55; opposition to, 32–34, 49–51, 61, 83, 102–03, 138, 149–50, 155; from East, 33–34, 37, 44–60, 71–73, 76–77, 86, 89–90, 102, 119–20, 123–24, 128, 154, 164, 168–69, 182; discouragement, 34, 50, 72, 83, 154–55; commissions, 49–52, 79–80, 82, 84, 131; relation to presbytery, 58–60, 90–91, 102, 114–18, 134; wives of, 68–70. *See also* Ministers; Missionary societies
Missionary Intelligence, 57
Missionary Reporter, 57
Missionary societies: 20–21, 30, 32–34, 37, 40–63, 102, 110, 119, 124, 129; motivation, 46–48, 55–56, 157; consolidation of, 48; journals, 55–57. *See also* American Home Missionary Society; Missionaries
Mississippi River, 1, 35
Mississippi Valley, 46–47, 109, 111, 157–58
Missouri, 77
Monfort, David, 73, 122, 127, 145; *Sermon on Justification*, 138, 140–43
Monroe County, Ind., 99 n., 178
Monticello, Ind., Presbyterian church, 79, 99
Moores, Charles, quoted, 170
Moores, Julia Merrill, quoted, 114
Moravians, 95, 190
Moreland, John R., 73, 104, 122, 125, 127
Morgan County, Ind., 164
Mormons, 185
Morrison, John I., 176
Mosquito (anopheles), 13

Mount Pleasant, Ind., Presbyterian church, 115
Muhlenburg (Ky.) Presbytery, 74
Muncie (Ind.) Presbytery, Minutes of, cited, 108
Music (church), 91, 96, 99 n., 105, 164–65
Muzzy, Sidney, 117–18

National Road, 4
Negro, 151–52. *See also* Slavery
New Albany, Ind., 112, 174, 186–87; Presbyterian church, 20, 44, 77, 84, 92, 98, 162, division, 129; Synod at, 109–10, 149
Newburgh, Ind., 176
New England, 31, 46, 56, 74, 82, 189–90; missionaries from, 37, 44, 49, 54, 71–73, 90, 120; church government, 45; Presbyterian theology, 119–20, 123–25, 128, 140–41, 145–47. *See also* East, Yankees
New Hampshire, 13, 131, 169
New Harmony, Ind., 5
New Haven, Conn., 184–85; Theology, 140
New Jersey, 172
New Lexington, Ind., Presbyterian church, 75, 85
New Lights, 124, 150
New Providence, Ind., Presbyterian church, 87, 109, 131
New Purchase. *See* Hall, Baynard
New School (Presbyterian), 34, 100, 102, 133; ministers, 73, 76, 122–28, 135, 146–47; doctrines, 119–21, 123–25, 128, 140–41, 143–50; paper, 128, 148; position on slavery, 152–53, 186; college, 183–85. *See also* Old School–New School division

211

✠ INDEX ✠